IRAN REFRAMED

Stanford Studies in Middle Eastern
and Islamic Societies and Cultures

IRAN
REFRAMED

Anxieties of Power in the Islamic Republic

NARGES BAJOGHLI

STANFORD UNIVERSITY PRESS
Stanford, California

STANFORD UNIVERSITY PRESS
Stanford, California

This book has been partially underwritten by the Stanford Authors Fund. We are grateful to the Fund for its support of scholarship by first-time authors. For more information, please see www.sup.org/authors/authorsfund.

Printed in the United States of America on acid-free, archival-quality paper

LIBRARY OF CONGRESS CATALOGING-IN-PUBLICATION DATA
Names: Bajoghli, Narges, 1982– author.
Title: Iran reframed : anxieties of power in the Islamic Republic / Narges Bajoghli.
Other titles: Stanford studies in Middle Eastern and Islamic societies and cultures.
Description: Stanford, California : Stanford University Press, 2019. |
    Series: Stanford studies in Middle Eastern and Islamic societies and cultures |
    Includes bibliographical references and index.
Identifiers: LCCN 2018059770 | ISBN 9781503608849 (cloth ; alk. paper) |
    ISBN 9781503610293 (pbk. ; alk. paper) | ISBN 9781503610309 (epub)
Subjects: LCSH: Motion picture industry—Political aspects—Iran. | Motion
    pictures—Political aspects—Iran. | Motion pictures in propaganda—Iran. |
    Iran—Cultural policy. | Iran—Politics and government—1997–
Classification: LCC PN1993.5.I846 B35 2019 | DDC 384/.80550904—dc23
    LC record available at https://lccn.loc.gov/2018059770

Cover design: Kevin Barrett Kane

Typeset by Kevin Barrett Kane in 10/14 Minion Pro

To my parents, Javad Bajoghli and Mahla Moazami,
who made this all possible.

Contents

Preface   ix

Introduction   1

1 Generational Changes   26

2 Cracks in the Official Story   50

3 Insiders, Outsiders, and Belonging   65

4 New Strategies   83

5 Producing Nationalism   100

Conclusion   113

Acknowledgments   121

Notes   129

Bibliography   141

Index   153

Preface

"During the war, we had to shed blood for the revolution, and we did. Later, we believed we should publish journals and books for the revolution, and we did. Today, we think cinema expresses [our ideas] best, so we make movies." These words were spoken in 2010 by Masoud Dehnamaki, a leading regime filmmaker, founder of the paramilitary Ansār-e Hezbollah in Iran and director of box-office-smashing films about the Iran-Iraq war. Dehnamaki gained notoriety for inspiring a "new entertainment" that communicated pro-regime messages to young audiences by appropriating forms of banned popular culture, such as music.[1] In his 2010 statement, however, Dehnamaki was not talking about technique. He was speaking of a wholesale shift in emphasis. For him, the quest to make revolutionary subjects was a struggle to be waged in visual media.

Men like Dehnamaki, who had dedicated their lives to the military and paramilitary apparatus of the Islamic Republic of Iran, found media such a powerful avenue to communicate their ideals and ensure the success of their political project that they turned from a life in arms to one on screens. Earlier, in 2007, I had read on Dehnamaki's blog that he and men from different pro-regime paramilitary organizations were planning on creating opportunities for the younger generation to make media. Given the increased economic and political power of the Revolutionary Guard, Iran's preeminent military organization, I wondered what this new effort by Dehnamaki and his col-leagues would look like and what the outcomes would be. "Culture" had been a prime battleground since the early days of the 1979 Revolution, so what would be different now?

I knew I would get formulaic answers if I pursued only formal interviews with these media producers. Like state elites the world over, they would stick to conventional answers. I wanted to understand these media producers in all of their complexities by spending prolonged periods with them at work and in their off-hours. Over a span of ten years, I gained access to regime media producers and the institutions they worked for, observing them closely as they developed new material to keep their revolution alive into its fifth decade.

Once I began my long-term research in Iran in 2009, I became immersed in the richly complex and competitive environment of regime media produc-ers. I found a media world in which men tied to the Revolutionary Guard and the country's paramilitary organizations held heated debates about the future of the Islamic Republic, fought with one another over resources, and pursued their projects through trial and error.

The men who appear in this book, as well as their families, challenged everything I thought I knew about Iran, revolutions, and states. Ultimately, this book is the result. It is a book not only about regime media but about the men who produce this media and what it means to doubt what they have fought for, not know what is to come, and be wrought with anxiety about the fact that they may be relegated back to the margins of society if their political project fails.

The story of how military and paramilitary media producers work on behalf of a state project raises important issues about politics, media, and revolutions. I have done my best to present these issues clearly within the nar-rative of the book. There is much more to be said about these issues beyond the scope of this book. I hope readers will forgive any omissions.

IRAN REFRAMED

Introduction

"**THIS YOUNGEST GENERATION** in our country doesn't understand our revolutionary language anymore," Reza Hosseini told his colleagues.[1] "We're wasting
our time with the media we make."

At forty-five, Mr. Hosseini had retired from active duty in Iran's preeminent military organization, the Revolutionary Guard, and now worked as a
writer, director, and producer of pro-regime content. In front of him sat seven
high-level officials of the Revolutionary Guard who oversee media production in the country. They met on a regular basis in a plain conference room
of a regime publishing house in central Tehran. A long oval table was surrounded with office chairs covered in their original protective plastic, which
had blackened from use over the years. Although the room was tucked away
from the pollution and heavy traffic outside, the incessant honking of horns
was still audible. A powerful air purifier made little difference, because the
sharp smell of exhaust seeped into the room. The tea service on the table was
growing cold, and sweets, like the tea, were left untouched. The men—still in
their black and grey winter coats despite the blast of heat from the heater—sat
silently, each staring off into space.

It had been just over three years since the 2009 Green Movement uprising—
the biggest mass demonstrations in Iran after the 1979 Revolution. Since
2009, the Islamic Republic's cultural producers had held numerous meetings

in which they contemplated what had inspired so many young Iranians to come out onto the streets and protest the government. The demonstrators decried perceived voter fraud during the presidential elections in which the incumbent, Mahmoud Ahmadinejad, was declared the victor just hours after the polls had closed.[2] Protestors believed that Ahmadinejad's Interior Ministry, with possible tacit support from the Supreme Leader's Office, had committed voter fraud to ensure that the highly popular reformist candidate, Mir Hossein Mousavi, would not win. What began with "Where is my vote?" turned into shouts of "Down with the dictator!" The slogans of the 2009 protests were eerily similar to—indeed many were facsimiles of—the slogans the men in the Revolutionary Guard remember shouting as young men against the Shah in 1979. How could young people on the streets in 2009 be mimicking their revolutionary slogans, but using them this time against their own revolution?

Mr. Hosseini broke the silence, as usual. "These kids don't care about the revolutionary stories we've told them the past thirty years, and it's our own fault. We can't blame them. We haven't properly communicated our stories to them. We need to bring them back to our side by telling better stories." Having grown up in Abadan, home to the largest oil refinery in the Middle East before the revolution, Mr. Hosseini prided himself on having had an upbringing surrounded by Americans, Brits, and Iranians from all walks of life. He didn't classify people into insiders (*khodi*) and outsiders (*gheyr-e khodi*), like many of his colleagues did when describing different social factions in Iran.[3] Mr. Hosseini made it a point to have close friendships with those who disagreed with him and the system he supported.

In these meetings, Mr. Hosseini was usually quick to argue that the Islamic Republic should be more flexible with young Iranians. "We keep pushing them away by making their lifestyle choices suspect and illegal. So what if they like to have spiked hair that reaches the sky and to wear skinny jeans? That doesn't matter, but we've turned these things into political issues."

Mr. Hosseini is typical of the first generation of Revolutionary Guard members. Having volunteered as a young man to fight in the war with Iraq that followed the revolution, he honed his skills on the battlefields of the twentieth century's longest conventional war. There, he and his fellow soldiers demonstrated their willingness to defend their country and their revolution to death. Today, he and some of his comrades from the war constitute the top echelons of the Revolutionary Guard.

"The protestors are not to blame," he said, again fixing his look to the corner of the room, his arms crossed on his chest, leaning back on his chair. His own wife and children had joined the protestors in 2009. After a silence, he continued, "We're the ones that need to adapt to the realities of our country."

Mohammad Ahmadi, a prominent film producer who directed one of the most notable pro-regime film collectives in the country, nodded in agreement and chimed in, "I talk about this all the time with my filmmakers. We've lost the youth in our country. We need to face this reality."

"But we can't give in to their demands! What do we become then, if we do that?" interjected Asghar Haghighi, a fifty-year-old general in the Revolutionary Guard. "We have to teach them the right way. Just because they demand something doesn't mean we have to give in to them. Do you do that when you discipline your own kids? No! So we shouldn't do that with the country's youth either!"

"Look, Asghar," Mr. Ahmadi said, turning his attention to his senior colleague, "if we don't become more flexible, we lose the entire system. The future is theirs because of their sheer numbers. They outnumber us. And not only that, if we don't become more flexible, we could turn into Syria."

"It's true," Mr. Hosseini interjected, suddenly becoming animated and sitting upright in his chair. "Our system has problems; which system doesn't? But we can't have our young people going into the arms of any opposition just because they dislike us. That's exactly what happened in Syria and look at the civil war that's begun there."

Later that day, Mr. Hosseini gave me a ride back from the meeting. Furrowing his brow, he said, "Maybe we were right in suppressing the Green Movement. If we hadn't, maybe we would've had the same situation here as in Syria." It was hard for him to voice those words. He and his close friends in the Revolutionary Guard had voted for Mir Hossein Mousavi, the reformist candidate. And more than that, they despised the incumbent president, Mahmoud Ahmadinejad.

His fear of Iran "turning into Syria" revealed a difficult truth that all my interlocutors in the Revolutionary Guard eventually voiced to me as the Syrian civil war turned bloodier and more complex. Syria became a metaphor for what Iran's military elite sought to avoid at all costs. Yet they also viewed Syria as the stage on which the wider regional and global wars for influence and power played out, and in which they were heavily involved.

For Mr. Hosseini and his colleagues, the international meddling in the Syrian war also resembled the Iran-Iraq War (1980–88). Though long forgotten in most parts of the world, the Iran-Iraq War continues to reverberate in the Middle East. Saddam Hussein invaded Iran just over a year after the success of the 1979 Iranian revolution and the establishment of the Islamic Republic. The bloody war, characterized by trench warfare and chemical weapons, dragged on for eight years. Though this was ostensibly a war between two nation states, most Arab countries supported Iraq, and regional and international powers played the two countries against one another. As Morteza Sarhangi, a prominent regime journalist and writer, said to me, voicing the official stance of the Iranian state, "This war was actually World War III. Over two dozen countries were involved in the war. Western powers wanted to see our two countries destroy each other so they could have influence in the Middle East and over our oil and resources."

For Iran's young soldiers, mostly volunteers in the pro-regime Basij paramilitary militia and the Revolutionary Guard, the war was not only their coming-of-age story but also the prism through which they viewed international relations. Mr. Hosseini and his colleagues understood all too well what it meant to be pawns in larger geopolitical power plays.

The next month, at a meeting with the same men, Mr. Hosseini said to his colleagues, "We can't have young people go into the arms of the opposition just because they want change. They need to know that we're not their enemy. But the Green Movement and our response in 2009 made them feel we're against them."

"Exactly!" Mr. Ahmadi jumped in excitedly. "We've distanced ourselves from young people and that's the real danger. God forbid one day Daesh (ISIS) or another group attacks Iran. Will our young people rise up and defend the country the same way our generation did with Iraq? If we keep distancing ourselves in this way, the answer will be no."

Alireza Shirazi, an executive in the state-run television network and a former officer of the Revolutionary Guard, agreed with Mr. Hosseini and Mr. Ahmadi, "We need to make sure young people don't feel dismissed by us. That's why managing our media correctly is so important." He leaned in with his elbows on the glass table and continued, "You all know our hands are tied at state television. We can't produce different media because of our restrictions. So it's up to the rest of you to create media that will draw young people closer."

"The first step is to stop producing the propaganda of the past three decades," Mr. Hosseini said. "We need to communicate in a language young people will understand."[4]

Mr. Ahmadi nodded his head and interrupted Mr. Hosseini. "Yes, and we need to stop framing our story as one that's just about the Islamic Republic," he said. "It needs to be about Iran. Our young people may not defend the regime because they don't feel a part of it, but they will rise up to defend Iran because they are nationalistic. So our media needs to center on Iran as the thing that we're all defending, not just a regime or ideology."

The other men looked on as Mr. Hosseini and Mr. Ahmadi made their point. "But people think everything we produce is propaganda," said Mr. Mohseni, a sixty-year-old Revolutionary Guard captain. Mr. Ahmadi drew his body closer to the table before responding, "That's why we need to make films that people don't think we made."

"We need to hide the fact that we're the ones making the films they see," Mr. Hosseini added.

Keeping a Revolution Alive

What does it mean to have the commanders of Iran's most powerful military apparatus, the very force in charge of defending the revolution, admit that the majority of the population no longer understands the regime's revolutionary stories? With the Islamic Republic entering its fifth decade, these men recognize that a sizable number of Iranians are tired of the state's propaganda, and because of that, the regime confronts a crisis of credibility. The guardians of the Islamic Republic now face the classic paradox of any successful revolutionary movement: namely, how to transmit the commitment to their revolutionary project from one generation to the next?

The 1979 Iranian Revolution, a massive popular revolution against the American-backed government of Mohammad Reza Pahlavi, ended millennia of monarchy in Iran and instituted the nation's first republic. Protestors and revolutionaries came from all political backgrounds, including leftists, liberals, Islamists, and Marxist-Islamists. The exiled religious cleric Ayatollah Khomeini commanded the greatest amount of support and eventually became the leader of the postrevolutionary government. The Shah fled Iran in January 1979. By February, Khomeini had triumphantly returned to Iran, and by March, the Islamic Republic was established by a popular referendum. In November 1979, students in support of Ayatollah Khomeini stormed the American Embassy compound in Tehran and took fifty-two hostages for 444 days, redefining Iran-U.S. relations to this day. A year later, in September 1980, Iraq invaded southern Iran and started what would become a bloody eight-year war between the two neighbors.

The 1979 Iranian Revolution reorganized the geopolitics of the Middle East. Iran had been America's most powerful ally in the region, and the Shah did the bidding of the United States in the Middle East. Given the fact that Iran shared a long border with the Soviet Union during the Cold War, Iran had become the pillar of U.S. foreign policy in the region, and it was rewarded handsomely for its cooperation. One of the main rallying cries of the 1979 Revolution was "Neither East nor West. Islamic Republic!" Iranian revolutionaries made it clear that they no longer wished to be ammunition in the larger political fight between the United States and the Soviet Union. Iran shifted from being a staunch U.S. ally governed by an autocrat who made claims of a "modernizing" state to one governed by Shi'a Islamic norms as defined by the anti-imperialist Ayatollah Khomeini.

In response, the United States overtly supported Iraq during the Iran-Iraq War, while covertly supporting Iran through the sale of arms, aiming for a war of attrition between the two sides. Iran helped found Hezbollah in Lebanon in 1982, and through direct military aid, the United States ensured that most Arab states in the region turned their backs on Iran. Once the Taliban and Saddam Hussein were toppled by the United States in 2001 and 2003, respectively, Iran saw its position in the region rise, as its two closest enemies no longer posed a threat. The 1979 Iranian Revolution had far-reaching reverberations in the region and the world, contributing to the rise of Islamist political movements and the proxy wars between Iran, Israel, and Saudi Arabia in Syria, Lebanon, Yemen, and Iraq, as well as the prolonged animosity between Iran and the United States.

The Iranian state's cultural producers debated their responses to the 2009 Green Movement in the context of these broader geopolitical transformations. As any revolutionary system becomes the status quo, it inevitably faces the challenges of safeguarding the revolution, as well as the socioeconomic and class status of its leaders, and appealing to younger generations and their demands for political participation. Scholars of revolution have long noted that the transformation of class systems in revolutions are crucial. The 1979 Revolution and the political system created afterwards fundamentally transformed the class system of the ruling elite. Regime elites in Iran currently ponder how to maintain the socioeconomic status that they gained through the revolution, while also making the system flexible enough to incorporate outside challenges. This balance has become increasingly delicate in the Islamic Republic, however, because audiences flippantly dismiss cultural material from the state as "propaganda." Regime cultural producers have come up with a threefold solution to this problem: first, hide the fact that the state supported, produced, or created the media through strategies of dissimulation; second, create new ways for audiences to see the media; and third, appeal to a populist nationalism as a unifying force that is "beyond" political ideology.

The new stories they tell the citizens portray the Revolutionary Guard (and the Islamic Republic by extension) as the only entity that can keep Iran safe and prevent it from falling into bloody conflict, like its neighbors. Yet, at the heart of these debates about how best to communicate with the public is contestation about how to define the political project of the Islamic Republic.

In this dynamic, everything becomes both a possibility and a problem.

The Regime's Intergenerational Divide

It was the third day of the massive Green Movement protests against the reelection of Mahmoud Ahmadinejad, a hot day just before the official start of the summer in 2009. The country was abuzz with excitement and anxiety. Ahmadinejad's detractors felt angry and betrayed. Yet, after the initial two days of vast protests in major cities around the country, there was also a palpable feeling of hope. Being a part of that immense crowd of humanity—marching alongside elderly men and women and young couples with small children—felt safe and wholesome.

Mohammad Ahmadi and his family had participated in the protests from the first day. Mr. Ahmadi was not only a prominent regime cultural producer, but also a visibly wounded war veteran whose legs had been blown off by a bomb during the Iran-Iraq War. He had voted for the reformist candidate, Mir Hossein Mousavi, and vehemently disagreed with the incumbent, Ahmadinejad. He was joined by his adult son, Mohsen, in his late twenties, who pushed his father's wheelchair proudly; his wife, Afkham; and their daughter, Laleh. Afkham and Laleh each wore a black chador—a full-length veil that covers the body, leaving only the face exposed—signaling their piety. The family protested on the first two days with no incident.

Buoyed by the energy of the streets, Mr. Ahmadi and his family left their home on the third afternoon. That day the protests became hairier. As Mr. Ahmadi and his family approached one of the main throughways with the throngs of protestors, they saw plainclothes paramilitaries attacking protestors. The young men, part of the Basij—the same pro-regime paramilitary group that Mr. Ahmadi had proudly joined as a fifteen-year-old during the war—were beating protestors with long black batons. They raised the batons high in the air before bringing them down with a vengeance on the bodies of protestors. Mr. Ahmadi saw two of the Basijis spot his family in the crowd. The two Basijis called over two others, and they ran toward Mr. Ahmadi's family, surrounding his son, Mohsen. They remained silent while their batons rained down methodically on his body.

Mr. Ahmadi yelled at them from his wheelchair, pleading for mercy. He raised his hand—which had lost three fingers in the war—and demanded that they stop beating his son. To shut him up, the Basijis turned on him, beating him until they knocked him out of his wheelchair. Afkham, his wife, cursed at the young men: "He's a veteran of the war! What are you doing? You wouldn't be here without him. Get off of my husband!" They pushed her

back. When they felt they had made their point, they backed off and continued into the crowd. Other protestors helped carry the bloody and bruised
Mr. Ahmadi to his car.

Mr. Ahmadi knew that the riot police and Basijis had singled them out because he and his family looked pro-regime. Having visibly pro-regime families
at the protests undermined the regime's official position that the protests were
"anti-revolutionary." Despite Mr. Ahmadi's disbelief, the youngest generation
of Basijis were beginning to turn on the first generation of men who had
joined the organization to bear arms for the country. The challenges of defining what the regime would stand for and of reconciling the varying points of
view from different generations of those loyal to the Islamic Republic came
into sharp relief after the Green Movement.

Though this beating was nothing in comparison to the wounds he had
experienced at the war front, Mr. Ahmadi sobbed uncontrollably that night.
He was unable to believe that men in the Basij, the same organization he had
fought for throughout his youth, had beaten his mangled body. And so, in
2012, when regime cultural elites such as Mr. Ahmadi, Mr. Hosseini, and their
colleagues decided to build a bridge to the younger generation of Basijis, Mr.
Ahmadi said he couldn't go and talk with them. The memories of what had
happened in 2009 were still too fresh for him and his family. Mr. Hosseini
volunteered to start the conversation.

On a cold winter day in 2013, I made my way through heavy afternoon
traffic to the campus of the Art University in central Tehran, just north of
Valiasr Square. The streets outside the campus gates were busy as usual with
shoppers, office workers, students, and residents. This area of Tehran, like
most of the city, had experienced significant growth since the revolution.
Heavy traffic was the norm, and the streets were jammed with automobiles,
motorcycles, and pedestrians. I was there to attend my first "Art Circle"
(halqeh-ye honari), a weekly meeting hosted by the university's Basij students'
organizations.

Created in the aftermath of the revolution, the Basij paramilitary or-
ganization (sāzmān-e basij-e mostaz'afin, literally the Mobilization of the
Oppressed) was charged with recruiting volunteer fighters for the battlefront.
This organization trained hundreds of thousands of men and women in the

use of weapons. By the late 1980s, some three million volunteers had been inducted, and one-third of them saw action on the military front. Today the Basij remain one of the most important sites of state power, citizen participation, and citizen control in the Islamic Republic. Yet their focus has shifted significantly from military warfare to a different kind of front: the culture wars carried out primarily in the arena of media production.

The Basij has chapters in universities across the country. The central headquarters of the Basij has tasked its university students with serving as points of control against potential student organizing on campuses, especially since the 2009 uprisings. Students who join the Basij at the university level follow the directives of the Supreme Leader's Office and see themselves as the vanguard protecting the state against anti-regime student activism. Almost without exception, these students are the most hard-line elements on university campuses.

Events like the Art Circle offered a good opportunity for Mr. Hosseini to try to convince the younger generations of Basijis of their new media strategy. The Art Circle took place in the university's main auditorium, a space usually reserved for large film screenings and special events. Students invited regime artists to the Art Circle, engaging them in two hours of discussion about their work. This time, as in subsequent meetings, about thirty students attended the meeting (seventeen women and thirteen men). The women all wore black chadors and the men sported short beards and gray or black buttoned-down shirts that they left untucked over dark slacks. As the students entered the auditorium, the women sat in the back rows. Men could choose to sit either in the front or the back, but always maintaining a respectable separation from the female students.

Mr. Hosseini and I had met prior to the event at a busy intersection, and we walked to the university together. He was determined to provoke the students, he told me. He wanted to push them hard to reconsider their tactics of intimidation and instead to follow the lead of the older generation of Basijis and Revolutionary Guard to create more conciliatory media that had the potential to reach a wider cross section of Iranians. After we walked into the auditorium, he went up on stage, and I went all the way to the back of the auditorium to blend in as much as I could with the female students.

After being introduced by the group's leader, Mostafa, Mr. Hosseini quickly jumped into his presentation and posed a series of questions, or riddles as he called them, for the students:

> Why is it that we, with this great Iranian-Islamic culture, this great Shi'ism, have so few followers? We've become like a storeowner who has merchandise worth millions, but sells no more than 10,000 toman monthly [$3 USD at the time]. Why? What is our problem? Is it the location where we've opened the store? Are we trying to sell ice cream in the middle of the North Pole? Where does our problem lie? Why do our revolutionary stories no longer have followers inside Iran?
>
> We put so much energy into our work. In particular, the official institutions of the regime pour so much money into our media production, but we don't get anything in return. We still don't have the numbers of followers we think we should have. We blame our own people for not following us. But we never think that the problem may be from our end! We're speaking on a frequency that no one can hear!

As he began to summarize the strategy that he and Mr. Ahmadi had brainstormed, Mostafa, the student leader who had made the introductory remarks, stood up and, pointing his finger angrily at Mr. Hosseini, proclaimed, "Your generation may be tired of confrontation, but not ours!"

Mr. Hosseini interrupted him, "Your generation's understanding of politics is all wrong. Why is it that before the revolution, 90 percent of women in our society wore chadors, and today 90 percent of women barely keep the headscarf on their heads?" Mr. Hosseini was referring to a trend of challenging the mandatory veil that had been imposed by the Islamic Republic at its inception. Women's dress is often used as a yardstick to measure the "success" or "failure" of the Islamic Republic by both pro- and anti-regime actors, and some women have challenged mandatory veiling since 1979. Today, many women, especially young women, wear their veils loosely, revealing a lot of hair, a far cry from the ideal female Islamic citizen the Islamic Republic attempted to create with the revolution.

Mr. Hosseini continued, "You have to admit that our work these past three decades has had many faults. If it didn't, you would not see this kind of reversal in people's values. Why is every part of our society changing and progressing except for you *hezbollahi* kids [*bacheh hezbollāhi-hā*, referring to very hard-line regime supporters, not necessarily members of the Ansar-e Hezbollah organization]?"

A female student interjected loudly, "We need to show who is right and just in these conflicts—and that's our side!" (For this student, "our side" was regime supporters.)

"What you all don't understand," Mr. Hosseini responded, "is that most of our problems stem from the fact that we've stopped communicating with the other side. The majority of our society no longer listens to us. *That* is what needs to change, and that can only change if we engage with the other side." The meeting continued in this heated fashion for another hour, with Mr. Hosseini repeating the same points and the students interrupting and exclaiming that there was no need to engage in peaceful dialogue with one's internal enemies—meaning those who oppose the regime from inside the country—when they knew themselves to be "right and just."

When the meeting finally finished and we walked out of the auditorium, Mr. Hosseini, exasperated, whispered to me, "See, it's these younger Basijis and hezbollahis who are our real problem. It's these kids who want to push us into a deeper division from the young people who were in the streets for the Green Movement. When I joined the Basij at the beginning of the war, it was a matter of life or death. These kids are just ideological. Look at how arrogantly they claim that our side is right. They wouldn't last a minute in the trenches in Abadan if Iraq invaded again right now."

It was six in the evening and the sidewalks were thick with tired pedestrians trying to make their way through a labyrinth of cars, motorbikes, and street vendors. As drivers beeped their horns incessantly and motorcyclists zipped past, often three to a motorbike, Mr. Hosseini turned to me and said, "These young Basijis don't realize that further distancing ourselves from the general public is what got us in this mess we now face. We need to reach out to the other side that is protesting us, not alienate them, as these kids want. You know what these kids' problem is? They don't know what it was like to be marginalized in society. They don't remember, because they were born after the revolution. All they've ever known is a system in which our side has been in power."

For the leaders of the Islamic Republic's armed forces what is at stake today is the defense of heroism in the face of dominance. These men and their families did not command respect in Iranian society before 1979. Not only did state policies of the Pahlavi monarchy formally marginalize religious families, but also the elite looked down on them. Explaining their continued loyalty toward the Islamic Republic, men of Mr. Hosseini's generation describe its creation as an event that gave them and their families a sense of purpose and a place in society. I often heard them wonder aloud anxiously whether they would be driven to the margins of society again if circumstances in the country changed.

Mr. Hosseini continued, "The younger Basijis and hezbollahis don't know that if we don't take care of this revolution, we'll be relegated back to the margins of society." He stopped in the middle of the crowded street as people bumped into us. "They don't know how quickly things can change."

Categories and Their Shortcomings

Throughout this research I have struggled with how to refer to the men who were my interlocutors. I went back and forth between "paramilitary producers," "regime producers," and "establishment producers." I decided against "paramilitary producers" because not all the media producers that appear in this book were part of paramilitary organizations such as the Basij or the Ansar-e Hezbollah; some of them also belonged to the Revolutionary Guard. I chose *regime* over *establishment* for a few reasons. The most important reason is that although some of my interlocutors were a part of the Revolutionary Guard, some were Basijis, and some referred to themselves as hezbollahis, their common denominator was their belief in the regime (*nezām*). Defending the nezam was their ultimate red line, and they often referred to themselves as *tarafdārān-e hefz-e nezām* (believers in the protection of the regime/system).

I heard over and over again in their debates with independent filmmakers, as well as in debates among themselves, "Criticism of the government [*dowlat*] is okay, but not criticism of the nezam." My interlocutors always made this differentiation between the government and regime. The government is the elected officials of the Islamic Republic, and in common parlance, usually the president and his administration. The nezam, on the other hand, is the

Islamic Republic as a whole. Despite the political usage of *regime* by some scholars in the West to refer in a pejorative way to non-Western governments, in Persian, *nezam* is not imbued with positive or negative markers. Thus, although my interlocutors—and indeed the men who make up the echelons of power in Iran—did not all agree with one another about how the nezam should proceed or what domestic and foreign policies it should pursue, they agreed wholeheartedly that the nezam of the Islamic Republic, as an entity, should continue to exist.

Similarly, scholars of Iran's postrevolutionary system have divided the often-fractious internal politics of the regime into that of reformists (*eslāh-talab-hā*) and that of hard-liners (or principalists or fundamentalists; *tond-ro-ha/usulgarā-hā*).[5] But this differentiation is not clear-cut, and reformist members of the Revolutionary Guard and Basij also referred to themselves as "believers in the protection of the regime" (*tarafdārān-e hefz-e nezām*). I witnessed established hard-liners become reformists over time, and I saw how self-described reformists adopted hezbollahi dress and language in certain settings to come across as hard-liners. I even witnessed them using their connections with hard-line colleagues to win political or cultural concessions. At other points, despite heated debates between reformists and hard-liners, I saw them unify to defend the regime in the face of U.S. aggressions. Some saw themselves as reformists and wanted the Islamic Republic to change in form, while others were more hard-line in their outlook, and still others rejected these labels altogether, simply defining themselves as believers in Ayatollah Khomeini's revolution. All of them were adamant in being "believers in the protection of the regime."

But, most importantly, I put all these cultural producers in the category of "regime producers" because they differentiated themselves from the independent (*mostaqel*) cultural producers of the country, who tend to oppose the regime. This differentiation between those who work to maintain the Islamic Republic (with or without reforms) and those who oppose it is a boundary that all my interlocutors accepted and employed in varying degrees.

In this book, my aim is to demonstrate that the various "pro-regime" categories are in fact fluid. In the evolution from the revolutionary movement of the late 1970s to the creation of a post-revolutionary state, the question of what the Islamic Republic as a political project should look like and who should define it has been continually debated. Statecraft is not a one-off project, and the Islamic Republic is not an exception. The state is always in the process of making, whether politically, socially, economically, or culturally. Moreover, divisions *among* the supporters of the regime, especially among different generations, are varied and deep. Despite popular conceptions, confrontations with Green Movement protestors are not the only facet of the "youth question" in Iran. A similar generational divide exists *among* those who identify as pro-regime, and it can often be a wide chasm. In all these divisions among those who support the Islamic Republic, the sharpest arguments often involve what the regime means today, how it should be defined moving forward, and who should have access to power.

Building Access

Gaining access to do long-term participant-observation research with regime cultural producers in Iran has its particular challenges, and it took me years to get the access I needed. From start to finish, I spent nearly four years (2005–2009) securing the introductions to do this research and another five years of regular visits (2009–2014) to get the necessary access for conducting long-term ethnographic fieldwork. The majority of my research took place during the second term of Mahmoud Ahmadinejad's presidency, in the aftermath of the Green Movement and its suppression. Due to the heavily repressive and securitized environment at the time, it became increasingly hard—and at times impossible—for me to audio-record interviews, take pictures, or video-record in certain locations. The crackdown on the Green Movement and the use of recording devices by the state to incriminate protestors made many anxious about such devices in the years following 2009.[6]

Although I did not have the idea for this research in mind at the time, I first met Basijis and members of the Revolutionary Guards in 2005 when I was living in Iran during the second term of Mohammad Khatami's presidency. Civil society still enjoyed relative freedom, and I had embarked on a project for one of Iran's foremost NGOs to create a nationwide database of local organizations to respond to natural disasters, such as the devastating earthquake of Bam, which just months before had killed more than 26,000 people. Through this project, I was introduced to the NGO that worked with survivors of chemical weapons in Iran, mainly veterans. After multiple meetings, including trips to different parts of the country to visit survivors, I began to work more closely on this issue, and it opened my eyes to the diversity of those who are pro-regime. Through this work, I eventually set up an oral history project to record the stories of the survivors, as many were slowly dying of cancer or collapsed lungs due to their exposure. I directed a documentary about survivors, *The Skin That Burns* (2012), produced in New York University's Culture and Media program. Throughout those initial years (2005–2009) of working with survivors, I met with hundreds of veterans and current members of the Basij and Revolutionary Guard. In getting to know them, I realized how grossly misrepresented and misunderstood they are, whether in media in the West, in the popular imagination of ordinary Iranians, or in academic scholarship.

The relationships I built during this work with chemical weapons survivors proved essential to my ability to carry out the research for this book. Specifically, the physicians who I worked with to establish the oral history project, veterans themselves, were key in introducing me to their friends who were regime cultural producers. Since I was an outsider—not only as an Iranian American but also as a nonsupporter of the regime—I needed personal introductions from people that the regime cultural producers trusted. The doctors and directors of veterans' organizations I had met in my previous work were willing to make these crucial introductions. The work I had done with the survivors was "proof" that I felt empathy for those who were pro-regime, even if I did not share their worldview.

Although I had grown up most of my life in the United States, I had spent nearly all my twenties living and studying in Iran. By the time I started my research, I knew Tehran like the back of my hand, could easily switch in and out of youth slang appropriate for my age, had mastered the pop cultural references, and understood how to go in and out of official spaces in Iran. It had become second nature to discern when to pull my headscarf forward and speak in "official speak" in government buildings or when I was with markedly pious men and women. And likewise, I knew when to pull my headscarf further back and push my way into spaces that were hostile to those with pious comportment. I had learned that instead of asking for official permission to do something—which would likely be denied—I should negotiate unofficial permission. By the time I started my research, I could "pass" for a native Tehrani.

Yet, passing was only a superficial option for me. Besides being Iranian American—already suspect enough—I also came from a political family. I am the child of a leftist father and a mother whose family was split between cabinet members of Mohammad Mossadegh's government and those who held high-ranking political positions for the Shah. My father and uncles barely escaped a raid by regime paramilitaries at their mother's funeral in Isfahan. Every leftist activist who was caught that day was executed later in the week under the orders of Sadegh Khalkhali, known as the "hanging judge" of the Islamic Republic. My parents' close friends had been executed in the political prisons of the 1980s. Our close associates in Iran have all spent multiple years in prison (both before and after the revolution), had been forced to live underground in the first years after the revolution, and have dedicated their lives to public criticism and political activism against state power.

My initial instinct was to pretend that this personal history did not exist. But I learned very quickly that failing to acknowledge my personal connections to Iran's past could be dangerous. In early 2009, I met with a veteran and influential member of the Revolutionary Guard who held very conservative political views. We had scheduled a second appointment at his office. But before the meeting, he called me on my landline number (which I had not given him), and he told me that he would come to see me at my home. "Let me give you the address," I said. "I already know where you are," he responded briskly and hung up. I only had about twenty minutes to calm my nerves and figure out what to do before he rang my doorbell. He had gone out of his way to intimidate me and send a message that he could find out information about me easily. I posed no threat to the regime or its supporters, but I knew the mere fact of being Iranian American and trying to talk to regime supporters was sufficiently suspect in Iran.

When he arrived, I started a practice that I then carried out with every regime supporter I met after that point. Before he could even open his mouth, I started, "I know you have doubts about me. My family left Iran when I was four years old. My father was a leftist. Many of his close friends were executed, and others imprisoned, right after the revolution. We left Iran because he could no longer stay. I grew up terrified of you all. But I have learned over the years that the story is much more complicated than I understood. I would like to hear your story in your own words."

No one in her right mind would tell a regime supporter with obvious ties to the intelligence community that she came from a "counterrevolutionary" family, especially during Ahmadinejad's presidency, which was characterized by large-scale suppression. But in the few panicked minutes before the man arrived, I had reasoned that if he had ties to the intelligence community or was an agent himself, he would already know this information. So, I asked myself, why not just offer it myself and prove to him that I had nothing to hide? I learned through that interaction that being brutally honest, even to the point of seeming naïve, helped dampen suspicions. If I was willing to disclose my father's political allegiance, which was considered an "enemy" background, then I could not be hiding much else.

This strategy helped, as did my near-native fluency in Persian and the fact that I could pass as a Tehrani. But in that all-male environment, my body language and style of dress marked me as an impious woman. I was willing to don a more religious head covering or even a chador to gain access for my research. However, I inevitably ended up drawing more attention to myself because of my unease in the chador, especially when I tried to keep it on my head and write notes at the same time, which was no easy task. Also, according to pro-regime standards, I was a woman who made too much eye contact and smiled too easily, as much as I tried to hold back.

Female Basijis do exist, and they tend to be very active in writing oral histories and memoirs about the war for the most prominent regime cultural center, Howzeh Honari. However, female Basijis do not partake in film production. Female and male Basijis gave the same reasons for their absence: the long hours and constant travel involved in filmmaking. Because I was the only female in the vast majority of the situations I encountered during this research, I knew I could never pass as a pious pro-regime woman. And given the state of Iran's internal and external affairs, trying to pass would only mark me as a potential spy. So, at the beginning of each meeting, I fully embraced my position and clearly explained where I came from and why I was there.

As a woman, I was sure to have access to certain kinds of conversations and information. Maybe a male researcher would have been included in some private conversations that were deemed inappropriate for me to hear as a woman. Yet, being a female researcher had its advantages. The war veterans took me under their wings as a daughter, tried to teach me about their world, and protected me in perilous situations. Among the younger men, I attempted to create a sibling-like relationship, although some of them remained uncomfortable about speaking to me, an unrelated woman of their age. Despite the challenges of access, during nearly ten years of conversations with members of the Basij and the Revolutionary Guard, I was able to go a long way toward my goal of understanding their stories from their point of view.

In many ways, even though my status as an American raised suspicions, it also opened doors. I noticed that my interlocutors gave more of their time to me than they granted to researchers from Iranian universities, most likely because of the prestige of American universities. But importantly, since I had not encountered the Basij regularly throughout my childhood and teenage years, I did not have the same visceral reaction to them that anti-regime Iranians my age have. Without those difficult memories of harassment on the streets or being policed in school, I had a distance from these men and what they represented that worked to my advantage. Although I disagreed with much of what I saw and heard, I could listen and observe without a sick feeling in the pit of my stomach, unlike my anti-regime contemporaries who had grown up in Iran.

It was not only Iranians who saw me as a potential national security threat, however; I faced a similar obstacle in the United States.[7] In the post-9/11 United States, conducting research in the Middle East or on Middle Eastern Americans and Muslim Americans has challenges.[8] American foreign policy in the region since 9/11 has been destructive and has created difficult circumstances for researchers. At the same time, attacks in Western cities by dual nationals claiming allegiance to such groups as al-Qaeda and ISIS have led Western governments to view immigrants and Middle Eastern diaspora communities through the lens of national security. Suspicion of dual citizens has a long history in the United States. The question of divided loyalties and fears of the "enemy within" have often resurfaced, especially in times of overseas wars. I was subjected to a long bureaucratic process that involved my university's legal team and the U.S. government. The level of suspicion was such that at one point an administrator from my university asked me point blank if I was a double agent.

The sanctions against Iran meant that I had to jump through many more hoops than if I had conducted research in a different country. And moreover, I faced the constant threat of my research being halted indefinitely by the U.S. government. Given that I was doing research with "specially designated nationals," the U.S. government's code word for "terrorists," getting permits from the U.S. government to do my research took nearly one year and cost tens of thousands of dollars in legal fees, paid by my university.

Methodology

The majority of my research took place in Tehran, although I made frequent and prolonged trips to the cities of Karaj, Abadan, and Ahvaz. My main field sites for this book were production studios, film and theater sets, classrooms; I attended production meetings and went along on promotional trips throughout Iran and internationally. I complemented this foundational ethnographic fieldwork with formal interviews, life stories, and informal conversations with executive producers, government officials in the cultural sectors, managers, directors, editors, translators, journalists, and film school students. Over the course of my research, I conducted formal or informal interviews with 200 individuals, all members of the Revolutionary Guard or the Basij, or both; 150 of those I interviewed had spent at least some time on the battlefront during the 1980s, while the other 50 belonged to the younger, third generation of Basijis.

I attended and observed the main film festivals in Iran, including the Fajr Festival (in both Abadan and Tehran) and the Cinema Verité Film Festival (in Tehran). I also attended smaller, ad hoc pro-regime festivals. I attended all public events on pro-regime media, making sure to cover a range of perspectives from within that world. I also attended events hosted by more independent cultural organizations. I attended pro-regime museums throughout the country, interviewed their directors, observed their public programming, and conducted informal interviews with their guides and employees.

I went on trips organized by regime centers to battlefields throughout the country in order to learn how they present the memory of the Iran-Iraq

War to their supporters. I was able to gauge audiences' responses to pro-regime films by interviewing audience members and observing two semesters of classes at the Art University in Tehran, where university students are taught some pro-regime works. At the Art University, in addition to observing classes taught by regime filmmakers to students who did not identify as pro-regime, I also attended one semester of meetings held by the university's Basij and Ansar-e Hezbollah students. I attended over fifty public events and twenty private workshops organized by independent artists who are against regime media producers. I also screened regime films for independent artists and activists in order to gauge their reactions. I sat in on interviews that historians at the Cinema House conducted with filmmakers and film producers, to gain an understanding of how film history is being written in Iran, as well as to observe the interactions between those affiliated with the Cinema House and regime filmmakers. Finally, I systematically collected a range of textual materials related to pro-regime-produced media. These include books by cultural producers, pamphlets, state press coverage of films and events, and non-regime media's coverage of pro-regime media and media makers.

The "media world" of the Revolutionary Guard and Basij includes television serials, documentary and narrative films, and dubbed and subtitled serials and films meant for export to Shi'a Arab countries via Iranian satellite stations.[9] I interviewed and did participant observation with directors of all the major regime cultural centers in Tehran, spending most of my time at Howzeh Honari, the largest and most important pro-regime cultural center in the country, and also visiting Sureh-ye Mehr and Revāyat-e Fath Center. I supplemented this time at cultural centers with long-term participant observation in five pro-regime film and television collectives, which included producers and filmmakers of various ages. My own filmmaking training and my native English made long-term research in these film studios possible. I was asked to help out in the studios in myriad ways and was eventually included in private meetings with cultural producers and local authorities about the media they were producing. In Abadan and Tehran, I also interviewed censors who targeted independent artists and sought to promote the work of regime media makers instead. I observed the regime filmmakers and producers who worked as freelancers to create content for state television. Many of the films broadcast on state television are contracted from these freelance film collectives.

Regime Media Producers' Stories

Although many people appear throughout this book, I weave together the stories of three individuals more often than others. They are the men I call Reza Hosseini, Mohammad Ahmadi, and Mostafa. I use pseudonyms for all my interlocutors in this book, except when I write about a specific filmmaker's work. Additionally, for these three figures, I have changed background information and certain employment details in order to protect their identities. Their stories best highlight the complex ways in which regime media strategies are created and carried out. But, more importantly, I share their personal stories to highlight for readers that the men who make up the regime's military and paramilitary organizations are not a monolithic group. In fact, they often disagree with one another and have conflicting ideas about how to keep their system going in the face of immense international pressure and domestic criticism.

Mr. Hosseini originally hails from the cosmopolitan port city of Abadan, in southwestern Iran. In its heyday before the revolution, Abadan was home to the Middle East's largest oil refinery. As a result, the city attracted a large number of American and European expatriates, as well as Iranians from across the country. Growing up in a pious middle-class family, Mr. Hosseini spent his childhood surrounded by books and movies from around the world. "I was fifteen years old when Iraqi bombs started to rain down on us," Mr. Hosseini recalled to me. "I remember I was on my way to school when I felt the first explosion. I had no choice but to get involved in the war. It literally came to my doorstep, and I had to defend my home."

Many veterans recalled the war with nostalgia, telling coming-of-age stories about the friendships they had made at the front in the face of danger. But for Mr. Hosseini, the war was much more than a rite of passage into adulthood. The war ravaged Abadan, and his family became internally displaced. His roots were violently torn out that ominous fall morning when Iraqi troops marched toward his home. Remembering the war and teaching future generations about it became Mr. Hosseini's life mission.

Although a staunch supporter of the 1979 Revolution and Ayatollah Khomeini, Mr. Hosseini credited his upbringing in Abadan among people of all different ethnicities, religions, and backgrounds for his ability to befriend people of diverse political persuasions, including those who were anti-regime. He prided himself on remaining independent among the different factions of the regime, and he never shied away from pushing the boundaries of what he thought was permissible because he found the boundaries too restrictive. He was one of my main interlocutors from the first and second generations of regime media producers, and he was also a leader in the regime media world.

Mr. Ahmadi hails from a working-class family in a central province of the country. He volunteered for the war at the age of fifteen, forging his parent's signature on the volunteer form and lying about his age. Only a few weeks after he landed at the front, a rocket pierced a truck he was riding in, blowing off both his legs. He arrived back home not only without legs but also—paradoxically—without many war stories to tell his curious friends. His town treated him like a hero, but soon his wounds healed and he faced the reality that he could no longer play soccer with his friends, that his family needed to carry him from place to place, that he would never be able to drive, and that he would be relegated to a wheelchair for the rest of his life. He recalled to me how he lay awake most nights wondering what his life would look like. He fell into a deep depression and refused to return to school.

Eventually, his family encouraged him to marry the young woman he had always had his eye on. Afkham was a distant cousin who lived in the same town and was only one year his junior. She and her family often visited Mr. Ahmadi's home after his surgery, and she continued to show interest in him. Young women were strongly encouraged to marry wounded veterans—it was seen as one of their contributions to the war effort. For Afkham, it was never a question. She and Mr. Ahmadi had stolen secret glances at each other since they were young teenagers. In time, they got married and, after they had their two children, Mr. Ahmadi's mood began to change. "My kids gave me something to live for," he told me. He decided not to finish his studies, despite the many opportunities available for wounded veterans to do so, and he took a full-time job in the media wing of the Revolutionary Guard. Once he had saved up enough money, he moved his family to Tehran and got a low-interest loan to buy a home in one of the new housing complexes the Revolutionary Guard had built for military families.

He began to work with Morteza Avini, the Islamic Republic's foremost documentary filmmaker. Although Mr. Ahmadi came into the media world of the regime a bit later than Mr. Hosseini, he has quickly risen in the ranks. Outwardly, he is more critical of the Islamic Republic than Mr. Hosseini. Being visibly wounded has meant that he is often at the receiving end of negative public comments about the regime. "Often, I can't go to the store or to work without at least five people giving me a dirty look or saying something about the political situation. I understand they're frustrated, but my legs were blown off when I was fifteen . . . I haven't been in decision-making positions for them to take out their frustrations on me!"

Mr. Ahmadi has grown unsure if giving up his two legs for this system was truly worth it. This sense of doubt and his experience of being a target for ordinary citizens' frustrations have made Mr. Ahmadi a willing leader among wounded veterans. He embodies the very complex, and often fraught, relationship that wounded veterans have with the Islamic Republic. But because he's risen in the ranks of the regime media world, he is also not willing to be a radical critic. His children are both highly educated and gainfully employed. They enjoy a much higher standard of living than their family members back in their home province. I witnessed Mr. Ahmadi carefully calibrate his criticisms based on who was in the room and saw him cater to the very men with political and financial power that he often criticized in private with other veterans.

Mostafa had been a leader in his university's Basij organization and is an emerging filmmaker in the regime media world. Although he had been born and raised in Tehran, his family hailed from the outskirts of the south central city of Kerman. He described his family as very traditional and was proud of the fact that his younger sisters wore the chador. His father was a car mechanic and his mother a homemaker. His parents moved to Tehran right before Mostafa's birth in 1994. They settled in the working-class neighborhood of Afsariyeh in southern Tehran. Mostafa was always a good student, and although his parents wanted him to become a doctor or engineer, he decided early on that he wanted to become a filmmaker. "I would spend all my time as a kid watching movies. Anything I could get my hands on. I dreamed of being a filmmaker, but we didn't have any equipment for me to practice with."

Although his family had lived in Tehran for two decades, most of their social life and network was still in Kerman. Mostafa's father, a believer in the Islamic Republic, encouraged his young son to join his high school's Basij organization to tap into a social network he could not provide him in the megacity. Luckily, one of the older Basijis at the neighborhood branch that Mostafa joined had dabbled in film and photography in the past. When he saw Mostafa's passion, he arranged to get camera equipment for him and introduced him to some regime filmmakers. Eventually, Mostafa landed a position at the Art University of Tehran. He told me he could never forget that if it weren't for his high school's Basij organization, he would not have been able to pursue his dreams.

My relationship with Mostafa and his family and friends took much longer to build than my relationship with his older colleagues. The fact that Mostafa and I were closer in age made holding meetings or arranging to see each other complex. As a pious man who also held a leadership position at his university, he had to be careful to make sure our meetings did not cross any religious or social red lines. Mr. Hosseini, Mr. Ahmadi, and nearly all of their colleagues from the first and second generation of regime media makers had children my age, making meeting with me less of an issue for them.

Because generational changes pose obstacles to creating new and appealing stories, revolutionary systems face the constant challenge of how to stay "alive." A revolutionary state like Iran contends with not only how to appeal to the younger people in the general audience but also how to build consensus among the younger generation within its ranks. In other words, a revolutionary state has the dual project of appealing to citizens while simultaneously defining what the revolutionary project, and its state apparatus, will mean over the long term. How to best achieve this goal, without losing the revolution altogether, is a contentious question. In these pages, I show how Mr. Hosseini, Mr. Ahmadi, and Mostafa, as well as my other interlocutors, grapple with it.

1

Generational Changes

ON A COLD WINTER AFTERNOON, I joined the directors of all the regime cultural centers in the offices of the Center for the Chronicles of Victory (Revāyat-e Fath). The center held pride of place in the cultural sphere of the Islamic Republic. Named after the influential weekly television documentary series aired in the 1980s, the center had been established by Morteza Avini, the godfather of postrevolutionary regime filmmaking.[1] The center continues to produce films that highlight the revolution, the war, and its martyrs. Some of those in the room had been members of Avini's original film crew during the war. All were men in their late forties and early fifties. Fervent revolutionaries in the first decade of the Islamic Republic, they now identified as reformists and lamented Mahmoud Ahmadinejad's reelection.

The center, right off Ferdowsi Square in central Tehran, was in the middle of one of the city's most crowded areas. By the time we had all arrived at the meeting, we felt like we had accomplished quite a task, getting there through the pollution, the endless crowds, and the aggressive Tehran traffic. We spent the first twenty minutes recovering, and the men caught up with each other. They congratulated one of the men whose daughter had been married the week before. They jokingly chided him for not bringing cake to celebrate with them.

At that moment, a man in his mid-twenties with an impressive beard and a black buttoned-up, collarless shirt walked in. The older men in the room were visibly uncomfortable, but they politely exchanged pleasantries with the young man. He asked the group if they needed his help in the meeting, and they politely declined his offer. As soon as he walked away, they gave each other knowing looks and a few shook their heads in exasperation. Mr. Ahmadi leaned in from his wheelchair and picked up his cup of tea. He took a sip and muttered, "Lā elāha ella allāh" (There is only one God).

I did not know it at the time, but this closed-door meeting was being held to discuss ways to limit the hand of Ansar-e Hezbollah and hard-line Revolutionary Guard members from the Center for the Chronicles of Victory. It would be a futile attempt, as the pro-Ahmadinejad elements eventually gained control of the center. The Supreme Leader's Office and the Ahmadinejad administration were determined to rid the ranks of anyone who supported the "sedition" (fetneh) of the 2009 Green Movement. Ansar-e Hezbollah and the more hard-line elements of the Revolutionary Guard began to insert their younger members into meetings at the center because it was a crucial node in the regime cultural sphere. Later, they ousted many of the filmmakers and producers who had been working there for years. The ousted included over half of those in the meeting that day, some of whom had been part of Avini's original film crew during the war and who were among the founding members of the center.

Three weeks after that meeting, Mr. Ahmadi received a phone call at home, just as his family was about to have dinner. It was from his boss, whom he had worked with for twenty-five years. Mr. Ahmadi recalled: "'They're changing things at the center,' he told me. 'It's best not to come back to work for a while. I'm sure this will be temporary.' I knew it wasn't going to be temporary. And just like that, they forced me out of the job I had done every day of my life for nearly three decades."

The tale of what happened to Mr. Ahmadi and his colleagues was a familiar one during Mahmoud Ahmadinejad's second term as president. After 2009, reformists were marginalized, and the government imposed repression in the cultural sphere and paranoia ran high. The international press widely reported that those who disagreed with the system altogether were imprisoned or silenced (e.g., renowned filmmaker Jafar Panahi). But what was not reported was how poorly the internal critics of the Islamic Republic fared—those who supported the system but advocated for an opening.

The films Mr. Ahmadi and his colleagues had in the pipeline to be aired on national television were pulled. Even more surprisingly, all of Avini's films, which had been the bedrock of the Islamic Republic for two decades, were confiscated from stores after the disputed 2009 presidential elections.

Mr. Ahmadi stayed home for three days after that phone call, but, he reported, "I knew I'd go crazy if I didn't work. I wouldn't let these kids silence us. They had already humiliated me during the protests. I wouldn't let them also take away my life's work." Knowing that he had all the right connections to get commissioned work, he decided to create his own production company. He hired five young directors and editors, and he busied himself with finding the assignments and the funding to continue producing films.

Before we get into the intricacies of the Islamic Republic's media world, some background is in order. To make sense of the current generational shift among regime supporters in Iran, we first need to look at the founding of the revolution.

The Revolution and the Regime's Military Forces

The 1979 Iranian Revolution, with its rallying cry of "Death to the Shah," came about through a vast mobilization of various sectors of society, and it resulted in the overthrow of millennia of monarchical rule and the institution of the Islamic Republic. Demonstrations against the autocratic rule of the U.S.-backed Shah began in the fall of 1977. With a wide range of groups initiating civil resistance campaigns, the protests intensified throughout 1978, including massive strikes that paralyzed the country. In January 1979, the Shah fled Iran with his family, and on February 11, 1979, Ayatollah Khomeini entered Iran from exile in France as the spiritual leader of the revolution.[2]

Despite the resounding victory of the 1979 Revolution, it is the 1980–88 Iran-Iraq War that provides the master narrative of the Islamic Republic. The revolution was too messy; it included too many secularists, leftists, feminists, and nationalists to be neatly packaged as an "Islamic Revolution," as much as the regime tries.[3] The war, which followed on the heels of the revolution, allowed the regime to imprison members of the opposition for reasons of "national security," to mobilize the population in defense of the revolution as the regime defined it, and to consolidate its power. In other words, the war crucially allowed the Islamic Republic to silence dissent, rally the country behind nationalist sentiments inherent to war, and strengthen the state.

In the years leading up to the revolution, Khomeini gained popularity by painting the Shah and the ruling elite as "morally corrupt," by being staunchly anti-imperialist, and by capitalizing on the class antagonisms between the lower class (*tabaqeh-e pāyin*) and the upper class (*tabaqeh-e bālā*), following in the footsteps of the anti-Shah leftist groups.[4] Khomeini and the core group of clerics who surrounded him vowed to right social wrongs by redistributing wealth and eliminating poverty, shantytowns, unemployment, and morally corrupt behavior. The establishment of the Islamic Republic relied upon the support of the *mostaz'afin*, members of the "dispossessed masses," who had indigenous organizing networks in mosques and neighborhoods. These networks served as organizing centers both to oust the Shah and to recruit volunteer soldiers in the subsequent war effort. It was this segment of the population that answered Khomeini's call to defend the nation and nascent revolution when Iraq invaded in September 1980.

Although both the Revolutionary Guard and the Basij were created following the 1979 Revolution, the Iran-Iraq War turned them into central institutions in Iran. With the once-powerful army of Iran in disarray and the new Revolutionary Guard still untrained, the Iraqi regime mistakenly believed that its invasion of Iran in September 1980 would lead to a swift victory. Instead, the 1980–88 Iran-Iraq War turned into the longest conventional war of the twentieth century. In it, trench warfare was used for the first time since World War I, and Iraq dropped numerous nerve-gas and chemical bombs on Iranian military and civilian populations, as well as on Iraqi Kurdish communities.

Iraq attacked Iran along its southern border, in the province of Khuzestan, home to Iran's ethnically Arab population. Saddam Hussein was hoping that Iran's Arab population would rise up against the Iranian government and side with the Arab invader, but that did not happen. Taking advantage of Iran's disarray following the revolution, Iraq made a surprise attack and quickly occupied the port city of Khorramshahr, twenty-two miles from Abadan. Iraq's eyes were on Abadan, where the Middle East's largest oil refinery at the time was located.[5] Despite a weakened army and an untrained Revolutionary Guard, Iran was able to fight off Iraq's assault on Abadan. It took two years for Iran to take back the city of Khorramshahr, at which point the Islamic Republic went on the offensive and attacked Iraqi territory under the slogan "From Karbala to Jerusalem." The war continued for another six years, and when both sides finally signed a United Nations cease-fire in 1988, no territorial changes had taken place.

The Revolutionary Guard

The founding of the Revolutionary Guard dates to the early months of the Islamic Republic.[6] Three months after the Shah fled Iran in January 1979, the Islamic Republic's Central Committee (*komiteh-ye markazi*) established the Revolutionary Guard with the mission of defending the revolution against "counterrevolutionaries," and the possibility of a coup d'etat. Reza, a former commander of the Revolutionary Guard, said to me, "In the days and months after the revolution, we woke up every morning wondering if the U.S. would stage a coup and bring the Shah back again, like they did with Mossadegh." The Revolutionary Guard was necessary because Ayatollah Khomeini did not trust the Artesh, Iran's professional army, which was a remnant of the Shah's regime. Khomeini believed the Artesh remained loyal to the Shah and could plan a coup d'état against him. Thus, while the Artesh would defend the nation—its territory and boundaries—the Revolutionary Guard was charged with safeguarding the revolution, both internally and externally, as outlined in Article 150 of the constitution. Between 1979 and 1980, the new government purged, dismissed, imprisoned, or executed 12,000 Artesh personnel. In total, between 30 and 50 percent of the officers between the ranks of major and colonel were removed. Additionally, approximately 60 percent of the army's original 171,000 personnel deserted after the revolution.[7]

Recruitment to the Revolutionary Guard began soon after its foundation, with many members coming from families who had belonged to the lower and lower-middle classes in revolutionary Iran.[8] Recruitment was primarily based upon recruits' ideological and political commitment to the Islamic Republic; only the most loyal citizens could join. Each potential guard had to pass a test on the Qur'an, the *Nahj al Balāgheh* (*Path of Eloquence*) by Imam Ali, and the *Hukumat-e Islāmi* (*Islamic Government*) by Ayatollah Khomeini as well as rigorous military and strategic tests.[9]

Importantly, the Revolutionary Guard, unlike the military in Syria and pre-2003 Iraq, is not controlled by one tribe, ethnicity, or family, but by people who remain loyal to the Islamic Republic. The Revolutionary Guard experienced exponential growth with the outbreak of the Iran-Iraq War and expanded its mission to include national defense.

At the beginning of the war, the Revolutionary Guard remained largely untrained and the Islamic Republic had to trust the Artesh to stave off the invading Iraqi military, effectively dividing the defense of the nation between the Artesh and the Revolutionary Guard. Despite the Revolutionary Guard's lack of training, Khomeini trusted it more than the Artesh. As a result, the Islamic Republic gave the Revolutionary Guard preferential access to arms and spare parts and better contact with the country's civilian leadership. During the war, it developed a structure parallel to that of the Artesh, with the creation of ground, naval, and air forces by the mid-1980s. The Revolutionary Guard also became instrumental in recruiting forces to the battlefront through the Basij paramilitary organization. By publicly framing the war as a struggle for Islam and the revolution, Ayatollah Khomeini and his government were able to counter the advanced training and weapons of the Iraqi forces with a surge of soldiers and manpower, many of whom eventually joined the Revolutionary Guard.

The Basij

In 1980, Ayatollah Khomeini launched the Basij, a volunteer paramilitary group in the service of the war effort; in 1981, the Sāzmān-e Basij-e Mostaz'afin (literally, the Mobilization of the Oppressed) became a unit of the Revolutionary Guard. The emphasis on this voluntary mobilization of the oppressed echoed the class-based revolutionary slogans of the 1977–79 revolutionary period.

In mosques and schools throughout the country, hundreds of thousands of men and women received training in the use of weapons. The Basij became the main channel to recruit legions of volunteers to the battlefront. Volunteers signed up for the war at their neighborhood Basij center. Each province in the country had at least one central Basij command center, while neighborhood mosques housed local Basij centers. For each new volunteer, a file was created, containing his photo and personal information, including parental permission if he was underage (many young boys forged these documents). The file also contained official permission for deployment (*barg-e e'zām*). For the first five years of the war, deployments were made individually, based on information the local Basij offices received about where volunteers were needed most. Starting in 1985, caravans of Basij volunteers in the thousands were sent to training and then the battlefront.

The Basij centers in each city and town coordinated their efforts and sent the volunteers to the Basij training center (*pādegāh-e āmuzeshi*) in their province's Basij command center for forty-five days of training. These forty-five days involved weapons and shooting training, body and strength training, and tactical and strategic training. The volunteers were taught how to fight both during the day and at night (most attacks by the Iranian side were done at night because they lacked sophisticated weaponry and could catch the Iraqis off guard in the dark), how to fight in the mountains and on flat land, and how to deal with landmines. Once trained, depending on the aptitude they had demonstrated during the forty-five days, some Basijis were then given specialties, such as reconnaissance, defusing mines, sniper shooting, while others were assigned general tasks.

In general, Basij volunteers were deployed from forty-five days to three months before they received a break from the front. Some Basijis renewed their deployment instead of taking leave, thus prolonging their service at the front. Anyone could volunteer to become a Basiji: young, old, man, woman. The women supported the war effort from behind the front lines as nurses and volunteers who made food and warm clothes for the soldiers. Men as old as seventy years volunteered at the front with the Basij, and although the legal age to fight was sixteen, younger boys eager to defend their nation forged their parents' signatures and were deployed to the battlefront.

Once a volunteer went through training and became a Basiji, he could be deployed to the front. If he desired to later become a member of the Revolutionary Guard, he made a formal request at a command center. The process to become a Guard was difficult and involved thorough background tests, including investigation of the applicant's neighbors and interviews about his family members, their politics, and their level of religiosity. Only after undergoing a lengthy investigative period could a Basiji with the right religious and revolutionary credentials become a member of the Revolutionary Guard. The Guard, as a more professionalized military force, received salaries of 70,000–80,000 rials per month (USD 777–888), compared to 20,000–24,000 rials per month for members of the Basij (USD 222–266).[10]

Both Revolutionary Guard and Basij members told me repeatedly how antihierarchical the warfront was; veterans remember fondly the sense of brotherhood and equality they felt at the front. Mr. Ahmadi recalled, "Sometimes our Guard commanders would wear the same khaki uniforms as us. They didn't want to differentiate themselves at all from us." Mr. Hosseini added, "We all addressed each other as 'Brother' [barādar]. I never recall addressing our commanding Guard officers in any other way." The sense of religious and revolutionary brotherhood prevailed at the battlefront, and men strived to create a feeling of equality among all those there, regardless of age, education, rank, or socioeconomic status.

For the most part, veterans told me that they had joined the Basij to defend the nation, its honor (nāmus), Ayatollah Khomeini, and the revolution. "I kept seeing news reports of our women being raped and killed in Abadan by the Iraqis, and I couldn't have lived with myself if I sat and did nothing. It was insulting to our honor [beh nāmus-emun bar mikhord]," Javad told me. He had volunteered at age sixteen from Karaj, west of Tehran. "I fought for my Imam [Khomeini] and to protect the revolution," said Mehdi from Arak, in central Iran, who had volunteered along with his three brothers, one of whom had been killed two years later on the front. "Our nation was under attack!" Abbas, a man from the Kurdish region of the country said. "I fought to defend Iran against those greedy Arabs." Honor, fierce nationalism, religious identification with Khomeini's interpretation of political Shi'ism, and the defense of the nascent revolution were the main driving forces of the tens of thousands of men who volunteered to fight at the front.

Defining Today's Basij

"The only similarity between the Basij of today and the Basij of the war is that we share the same organizational name. Those in the Basij today are horrible," Mehdi Kermani, a war veteran and filmmaker said to me one day as we sat sipping tea in his office in Revolution Square, steps from the University of Tehran's main campus. Mr. Kermani had worked at the Chronicles of Victory since 1989. He had also been pushed out of the center like Mr. Ahmadi. But unlike Mr. Ahmadi, Mr. Kermani had found the environment in Iran too suffocating after the 2009 suppression and decided to leave rather than open his own production studio. He was spending most of his time in Lebanon, making films with Lebanon's Hezbollah media team. He came back for short stints in Tehran to see his family and friends. "We're all so embarrassed," he said and then stared off into the corner of the room, his right hand mindlessly spinning a sugar cube on the glass table, his jaw tight.

Breaking his silence, he continued,

> Basijis used to stem from the people. The Imam [Khomeini] meant for us to serve the people and the nation when he created the Basij. But what they did this past summer [2009 Green Movement] was disgusting. They turned everyone against us.
>
> It's so painful that people think of the Basij in negative terms now. We were created for a different purpose at the beginning of the revolution. We went to defend the country against the invading Iraqi military, not to get better jobs or get into university, like the Basij of today. Or to beat our own people, for God's sake! When we became Basijis back then, we knew we could die at the warfront. We went because we really believed, so much so we were willing to sacrifice our lives. But not today. Today these kids are opportunistic.

Mr. Kermani's cell phone rang. It was Mr. Hosseini on the line. He was in the neighborhood and wanted to see if we would grab lunch with him. One of his favorite sandwich shops in the city was on the same street as Mr. Kermani's office. We picked up our things and joined him.

Mr. Kermani filled in Mr. Hosseini on our conversation. Mr. Hosseini turned to me as he took a bite of his kabob sandwich and said, "I'm embarrassed to tell you that I don't know what the Basij is today." He had spent all morning in an editing room, where the filmmakers were putting the finishing touches on yet another narrative film about the ways in which the newly minted Revolutionary Guard had suppressed the Kurdish uprising in 1980.

Mr. Hosseini stared off into the corner of the restaurant as he chewed on his sandwich, looking for words to define an organization that he had joined with conviction as a fifteen-year-old. He shook his head, as if in disbelief, before turning his attention back to his sandwich. Mr. Hosseini could no longer define the Basij, much less defend it: "During the war, everything was clear: the Basij was a training ground. But today, I honestly can't tell you what it's about."

"There is not one definition of the Basij. I guess we all believe in the Imam [Khomeini] and the revolution, but beyond that, we're mixed. And this new generation of Basijis," he scoffed, "forget about them."

The Question of Generations

Studying generational change has long posed a problem for social scientists, and how to classify generations remains a contested issue. Central to understanding the generational shift that Mr. Hosseini and Mr. Kermani alluded to is the work of Karl Mannheim. In his still influential study "The Problem of Generations" (1928), Mannheim shows that people are influenced by notable events that involve them actively in their youth—what he calls "fresh contact." These experiences lead them to become agents of social and cultural change, shaping future generations. But the question of how political ideologies are resignified and restaged over time is of interest more broadly across the social sciences, beyond the Iranian case.

In postrevolutionary Iran, generations are largely defined and culturally marked by the decade of birth, such as *daheh-ye shast, daheh-ye haftād* (the '80s generation, the '90s generation). Yet, that categorization does not extend to the war volunteers.[11] Because they joined at different ages, they are not categorized by their decade of birth but instead are referred to as collective groups that stand for generational units: "the battlefront guys" (*bacheh-hā-ye jebheh*) or "the guys of war" (*bacheh-hā-ye jang*). I categorize the first generation of Basijis, even if they came from different age groups, as those who fought in the Iran-Iraq War. The second generation is men who were too young to serve at the front but who joined the Basij in the 1990s. This second generation was instrumental in the postwar efforts of the organization, especially in the Basij postwar cultural campaigns. Some of the men in the first and second generations then joined the Revolutionary Guard. The third generation is those who joined the Basij around 2005—the year Mahmoud Ahmadinejad was elected president—under a new framework designed by the Supreme Leader.

Postwar Realities and the Changing Battlefront

When the war ended and there was no longer a need to send men to the front, both the Revolutionary Guard and the Basij had to recalibrate and demobilize. Although Ayatollah Khomeini's will banned the military from involving itself in politics, shortly after his death in 1989, the Revolutionary Guard not only got involved in politics but also became the main contractor for rebuilding the infrastructure of the country after the war. This turned it into the wealthiest independent institution in the Islamic Republic.

In his will, which serves as a manifesto for the post-Khomeini Islamic Republic, Khomeini wrote:

> My firm advice to the armed forces is to follow the regulation of non-interference of the military in the affairs of political parties. The armed forces, including the army, police, the [Revolutionary] Guard, Basij, and others, must not enter any political party and must keep themselves away from political games. Since the Revolution belongs to the people and its protection is the duty of all, it is the patriotic and Islamic obligation of the government, the people, the Defense Council, and the Majles, that if the armed forces, whether the commanders and higher ranks or the lower ranks, act against the interest of Islam and the country or if they want to enter political parties or political games, which undoubtedly will ruin them, they must be opposed from the very beginning. It is the duty of the leader and the Guardian Council to forcefully prevent this sort of action so that the country will be safe from harm.[12]

Due to the changing social, political, and economic conditions of postwar Iran, then-president Hashemi Rafsanjani (1989–1997) enacted policies that effectively transformed the Revolutionary Guard and allowed it gradually to infiltrate the economic and political life of the Islamic Republic.

With the increased presence of the Revolutionary Guard in various facets of the state's socioeconomic life, the Basij has become one of the most important sites of state power and citizen participation in the Islamic Republic. It is the Revolutionary Guard's primary apparatus for organizing and controlling the Iranian population through neighborhood branches, universities, factories, and workplaces.[13] Since its establishment in 1980, the Basij has collaborated with various police enforcement agencies in an effort to exert moral control over society. It has participated in law enforcement (at times specifically targeting dissidents), organized public religious ceremonies, provided emergency management and social services throughout the country, and produced media—all with a "proper" revolutionary and Islamic twist.

Khomeini's successor as Supreme Leader, Ali Khamenei, has allowed the Revolutionary Guard to enter politics in order to safeguard his own power. Khamenei, who does not enjoy the mass support and following of his predecessor, has appointed large numbers of former Revolutionary Guard members and commanders to political positions. Although the Revolutionary Guard has gradually entered politics since the end of the war, it came to play a large role in Mahmoud Ahmadinejad's administration (2005–2013): his cabinet and senior administrators either came from military, intelligence, security, or prison administration backgrounds or served as officers of the Guardian Council—the unelected clerical body empowered to overturn acts of the Majles (parliament). The Revolutionary Guard's involvement in business and politics has made it a powerful, independent institution within the regime.[14]

In the initial postwar period, the Basij aided in the moral policing of the population. Its members reprimanded women for not covering themselves properly. Also, they stood at street checkpoints to monitor for "indecent" music and behavior, as well as anything else that was deemed immoral. Following the death of Ayatollah Khomeini in 1989, the new Supreme Leader, Ali Khamenei, made the Basij one of the five main divisions of the Revolutionary Guard and shifted its mission to being a force responsible for the internal security of the state.

The Supreme Leader began to alter the Basij drastically when over half the Revolutionary Guard and Basij voted for reformist Mohammad Khatami in the 1997 presidential elections. Khamenei saw this large vote for reform from within the ranks of the regime's military and paramilitary apparatus as a direct threat to his rule. The Supreme Leader's Office, along with more conservative members of the Revolutionary Guard and Basij, decided to intensify the training programs, especially for the younger members, in an attempt to create a more loyal cadre of supporters within the regime's armed forces—ones who would not seek to reform the system. New ideological classes were added to the Basij training programs.[15] These new classes represented an intense effort in training and education about the Islamic Republic and Islamic society in accordance with the Supreme Leader's interpretations.

The goal was to create a stable voting bloc for more hard-line candidates and to avoid landslide victories of reformists, as in 1997. These foundational changes are a main reason that the younger generation of Basijis tend to support the Supreme Leader, whereas the war generation tends to support Ayatollah Khomeini and his family, who have become reformists. It was this younger generation of Basijis who was called upon to suppress the Green Movement and to "cleanse" the ranks by getting rid of the reformist members.

In postwar Iran, Basij members are divided into three groups: (1) regular members, (2) active members, and (3) special members. Regular Basijis are those who join, obtain a Basij card, and pass basic training. These members have little or no connection with the main Basij bases. Some of these members whom I interviewed became regular Basij members because they felt that doing so would allow them to scale the social ladder, helping them get into college or land a job. Some, especially those in high school (both boys and girls), had to join in order to go on certain field trips. They enrolled to receive the Basij card but then did not partake in any Basij activities once their field trip was over. The second group, the Active Basij members, are regular members who have engaged in at least six months of continued activity and passed training.[16] The third group, the Special Basij members, are those who have undergone military and ideological training and are technically members of the Revolutionary Guard. These Special Basij members are core members of the Basij organization and serve the Revolutionary Guard full time. They receive a salary for their work.

Yet, despite this attempted institutionalization in the postwar period, the Basij continues to have a loose structure on the ground. Basijis have a difficult time defining their exact role, and within their ranks I found great discord. The only Basij branch that tends to be unified is the one in universities. Otherwise, the current Basij members who serve in offices, factories, and neighborhoods are often unsure of their exact role. Most revealed to me that they had joined for upward social mobility or job stability.

Confronting Soft War

The vast majority of the Basijis' energies are expended in confronting "soft war" (*jang-e narm*), a term that is used loosely by Iranian officials to refer to the ways in which the United States, European powers, and Israel influence Iranian politics with the soft power of culture.[17] The current Supreme Leader, Ayatollah Khamenei, has repeatedly discussed the need to "vaccinate society" (*vāksineh kardan*) against the soft war that the West and the Iranian diaspora wage against the Islamic Republic.[18] As of 1994, 300,000 Basij had been recruited solely for the purpose of confronting cultural invasions, both from abroad and from within the country.[19]

Soft War and Psychological Operations, an initiative of the Supreme Leader, publishes reports on soft war activity against Iran and creates films and books to raise awareness and to train pro-regime experts to counter the soft war. Specifically, this initiative seeks to awaken Iran's youth to the threat posed by this soft war, to publish reports that help readers understand the nature of the enemy's strategies, to uncover the intricacies of the enemy's tactics, and to provide strategies for battling this soft war.[20] After 1988, the front line moved from the battlefield to the field of culture.[21]

This initiative became clearer for me the more time I spent with members of the third generation of Basijis. One winter afternoon in 2014, I was at a small film unit of the Basij with Mostafa. Mostafa was one of the leaders of the Art University's Basij Students' Association who had invited Mr. Hosseini to the Halqeh-ye Honari (Art Circle) event (described in the Introduction). He was one of the main students who had challenged Mr. Hosseini. Since that event, I had slowly gotten to know Mostafa.

In his last year at the university, Mostafa had begun working at a Basij production studio. He invited me to his studio to see his film work from time to time. The film unit Mostafa worked in was technically an independent studio, but it received a steady stream of assignments from different state television channels. He and two of his colleagues had been students in the same class at the Art University. The other five filmmakers in the studio, also graduates of the Art University, were slightly older than Mostafa. All the filmmakers in the studio had been members of the university's Basij association. Their boss, Alireza, was a producer who had strong connections to the central headquarters of the Basij.

That day, Mostafa had been busy editing his latest short piece for the Qur'an Channel, a state television channel that often commissioned work from studios like the one Mostafa worked in. When our eyes became tired after hours of looking at the two large screens in front of us, Mostafa went out to the kitchen and brought back tea and sweets for us. Ali, his classmate from the Art University and his colleague in the university Basij association, came into Mostafa's office carrying his laptop. Ali was hard at work on an editing project, too. His producers had tasked him with making a program for state television, a short sequence about American media and its opposition to the Islamic Republic. Every time he found something amusing, he would bring in his laptop to share it with us.

He showed us his latest find, a segment on CNN about why the Revolutionary Guard is so powerful in Iran. Like other American depictions of the Revolutionary Guard and of the paramilitary Basij organization, this segment portrayed Iran's armed forces as a homogenous-looking crowd of bearded men with stern faces dressed in fatigues or black button-down shirts, usually armed, listening to a speech by the country's Supreme Leader.

Mostafa and Ali watched it with wide smiles on their faces. When the short segment ended, Mostafa turned to me and said, "It's funny to me how Westerners depict us. They make it seem as if the Leader [Khamenei] says something and we just fall in line," he laughed. "Does anything in Iran work so smoothly? They should come and see how messy everything is here. What makes them think that amidst everything barely functioning—from our economy to our traffic to our work culture—that the Basij are so well-organized?"

"You're being optimistic to think that it's only foreigners who think this way about us," Ali responded. "Our own population thinks we're blindly ideological and out to make their lives hell."

"That's because of all the lies the Iranian stations from abroad tell them. And our people are misguided to watch these shows and read these websites," Mostafa responded with conviction in his voice. I pointed out the Radio Farda website open on his browser behind the Adobe Premier editing software window. "We have to know what they're saying in order to respond to it," he shot back quickly, minimizing the window on his screen before changing the subject.

Media from the Diaspora

Throughout my research in regime media studios, what always caught my attention was the fact that in nearly every regime studio the media producers consumed banned and censored media, especially from the Iranian diaspora. Radio Farda, in particular, was a popular program among regime media producers. The station is the Persian-language branch of the U.S. government-funded Radio Free Europe/Radio Liberty. Broadcasting twenty-four hours a day from its headquarters in Prague, the radio station began in 2003 as a joint effort with the Voice of America's Persian service. Although the Islamic Republic has condemned the VOA service since its inception, it is more tolerant of Radio Farda, even turning a blind eye when Iranian politicians do interviews with the station. My interlocutors said that they liked its format, which gives the top headlines of the day, and they appreciated the reporting it provides. As soon as important news broke, they would immediately turn to Radio Farda's website and stream its service. They did not view it as "pure Western propaganda" like VOA, BBC Persian, and Manoto, they told me.

The flood of Iranians escaping political, ethnic, and religious persecution following the establishment of the Islamic Republic created a thriving diaspora throughout Europe (especially Sweden, France, Germany, and the United Kingdom), Australia, and North America (in Persian, Los Angeles is colloquially referred to as Tehrangeles, and Toronto as Tehranto). Though not all those who put down roots in new places had left for political reasons, exiled political and social activists have created a dynamic media presence outside of Iran.

Prior to the 1979 Revolution, the Iranian Students' Confederation was the largest Iranian student group in the world.[22] It published regular pamphlets, newsletters, and newspapers. The Mujaheddin-e Khalq organization (MEK), the National Front, and the Tudeh Party also maintained an active media presence outside and inside the country. Iranian media beyond the country's national borders played a large role leading up to the revolution, and since 1979, they have become as much of a thorn in the side of the government as they were for the Shah. The biggest difference today, however, is the vast amounts of funding available from various Western governments for these stations and media sites.

Following the establishment of the new postrevolutionary government, exiled political activists built on these preexisting student and activist networks to re-create pressure points against the new government. Various political groups organized rallies throughout the 1980s to raise awareness about the suppression of political activists in Iran, and they held weekly meetings throughout Europe and North America, where news from Iran was shared and strategies for opposing the Islamic Republic were discussed. Eventually, as the Islamic Republic became a more permanent reality, groups debated how it had come to be and how it had grown such strong roots in the country.

In the 1980s, with Iran increasingly isolated from the outside world and with a bloody war under way, getting information and news in the diaspora in a timely manner proved difficult. International phone calls to the country were expensive, and families were too afraid to write anything political in letters. The MEK, which boasted a large underground presence inside the country at the time, created a radio news program that was accessible by phone. Even exiles who did not agree with the MEK called in to listen.[23] In other locations, on television programs created by and for Iranian exiles, some of the programming was dedicated to news and information sharing.[24] Newspapers and newsletters were produced in various cities in Persian, and publishing houses were established in major Iranian diaspora hubs, including Los Angeles, Washington, DC, Paris, and Stockholm. These publishing houses have played a crucial role by publishing books that have been banned in Iran, and importantly, they have published memoirs of political prisoners imprisoned in the Islamic Republic, giving an insider's view of the political suppression following 1979.

Given the experience of the revolution and its violent aftermath, the various media outlets throughout the diaspora are fractured along political lines, with some advocating for the return of the monarchy, while others serve as mouthpieces for the MEK, leftist groups, secular republicans, or others. Despite the fractured nature of the diaspora in its first two decades, the activities of exiles proved threatening to the government in Iran. In the 1980s and 1990s, the Islamic Republic notoriously targeted exiles in Europe, murdering dissidents in Germany and France. Following the eruption of the Green Movement in 2009, a new generation of political and social activists was forced into exile, and reports of intimidation by the Islamic Republic's security forces against refugees, especially in Turkey, demonstrate that the regime's tactics to stop its opposition continue. With the Islamic Republic's fierce crackdowns on internal newspapers and journalists, the newer news channels abroad that broadcast in Persian—such as BBC Persian, Radio Farda, Manoto, and Iran International—employ journalists who are no longer allowed to work domestically.

Diasporic satellite stations have been beaming programming and news from Los Angeles to Iran for over two decades. Although satellite dishes are illegal in Iran, families began to purchase them in the mid-1990s. Authorities frequently raided houses and rooftops in the 1990s and 2000s, but as satellite dishes became smaller and cheaper, more and more households began to own them. Though raids to confiscate dishes continue, they are less frequent, and the fight against satellite dishes seems almost futile, because there are now too many dishes in homes to control.

As the number of households able to access satellite programming has increased, the variety and quality of programming has grown exponentially in the last decade. The early Los Angeles–based programs have been superseded by big-budget stations spread throughout Europe and the United Arab Emirates. Popular Turkish soap operas are dubbed by Iranian actors in Toronto and beamed into Iran on the channels GemTV and River; Latin American soap operas are broadcast on Farsi1. The Saudi-based MBC channels broadcast Hollywood films and American shows subtitled in Persian. The BBC began broadcasting its high-quality Persian news service in January 2009; and Manoto, broadcast from London, offers a variety of shows from news to talk shows to Iranian diaspora competitions and reality shows, to dubbed British shows such as *Downton Abbey*. A plethora of stations broadcasts Iranian and international music videos. Additionally, the Los Angeles political and cultural stations continue to broadcast into Iran, as does a television station maintained by the MEK, as well as the Voice of America's Persian service, despite its deteriorating production values. These satellite stations exist alongside radio stations that broadcast from abroad into Iran, including BBC Radio, Radio Israel Farsi, and Radio Farda.

These media are augmented by Persian-language news websites and blogs. Until around 2009, Persian was the third most-used language on the internet. Prolific and sophisticated news websites of all political stripes publish material daily and play an active role in disseminating news the Islamic Republic would rather keep private. As of late 2018, Gooya.com, the main hub and directory of Iranian news online, offered links to 153 news sites maintained in Iran and the diaspora that were updated daily.[25]

Some of these news sites and internet-based human rights organizations have received funding from European and North American states. In 2007, President George W. Bush famously offered $75 million for promoting democracy in Iran, and funding for Iranian "pro-democracy" organizations continued under President Obama's administration. Some of the money went to establishing human rights organizations and blogs as well as news sites. The Trump administration increased the use of subversive state funding to satellite stations, as well as creating social media campaigns to further foment discontent against the regime. European countries such as the Netherlands and Germany have supported the establishment of news sites in Persian, and foundations such as the Open Society have offered funding for others.

This political and financial support, as well as the popularity of social media sites and mobile messaging apps such as Telegram, has prompted the Supreme Leader to demonize diaspora media and accuse it—and Western media more generally—of waging a soft war with fake news and disinformation campaigns meant to sow discord among the population. Although many websites are filtered in Iran, the *filter-shekans* (filter breakers) have become better at breaking through the Islamic Republic's filters and allowing users to access these sites. Nonetheless, as of 2016, the number of Facebook users in Iran was only 4 million due to state surveillance, while the number of Iranians using Telegram was 21 million.[26] Instagram remains unblocked in Iran and is the most widely used social media application. To counter this soft war, the Supreme Leader has tasked the Basij with "vaccinating" youth against these media platforms.

The relationship between regime media and diaspora media is fluid. On one hand, they harshly criticize one another in their programming, but on the other, regime producers watch the satellite stations for content ideas. Mostafa's producer, Alireza, said to me, "Stations abroad can air things that our misguided young people want to see. So I tell my filmmakers to watch that material for research. I let them watch it freely. Then I tell them, 'Let's adapt what they do, but within our values.' Iranians abroad produce corrupt content. We can produce entertainment that is morally correct. It's hard, but it's doable."

The Question of Class in the Basij

Like the first generation of Revolutionary Guard members, a great majority of Basij volunteers came from lower-middle-class families and some from middle-class families who tended to be religious. Only a few came from landowning families. "Dr. Hasani is the only rich kid I knew at the front," Mr. Saedi told me, referring to a physician who volunteered from the central town of Arak and came from a wealthy landowning family. Mr. Saedi, a sociologist employed by the research wing of the Revolutionary Guard, was especially interested in questions of class. According to the data that he and his team had gathered, the vast majority of those who had joined the Basij and Revolutionary Guard during the war came from humble backgrounds.[27] This correlated with my own findings. Many wealthier or less religious families tried to send their sons abroad to avoid recruitment to the front, despite the closing of Iran's borders and the extreme difficulty of securing visas for young Iranian men at the time. Veterans I interviewed asked me if my family left Iran in the middle of the war because my father was trying to avoid recruitment. Even today, there exists a division between those who voluntarily fought in the war and those who left the country.

Many of the men from the first two generations of Basij aspire to have their children rise in class position. Therefore, they keep them from joining the Basij as active members, whom they view as lower class. In essence, the divide, and often the disdain, that underlies the ways in which the first and second generations of Basijis speak about the third generation points to issues of status and class, as well as disapproval of the opportunism that they believe is the primary motive of the younger generation in joining the Basij. Although Mr. Hosseini, Mr. Ahmadi, and their cohort of first- and second-generation Basijis hail mostly from humble backgrounds, today they tend to inhabit comfortable middle-class lives. This pattern is different from that of Revolutionary Guard members who partook in business opportunities following the war that made them rich. Those men and their families now lead upper-middle-class lives.

Not a single first- or second-generation Basiji I met has allowed his son or daughter to become active in the Basij.[28] When I asked why, the response was nearly always the same: "There's no reason for them to be involved. And the atmosphere is not one I want my kids to be in." For the first- and second-generation Basijis, allowing their children to be a part of the Basij would be a step down the social ladder they have scaled. Instead, members of the first generation tend to save their money and send their children on tours of Europe. Although they perform their religious duties and go with their children to Shiʻa pilgrimage sites in Iran, Iraq, and Syria, they work hard to ensure that their children, both male and female, get a chance to travel to Europe once they are in their early twenties. Their children go on these trips with either their mother or an organized tour with other friends' children. A European tour helps ensure that their children have the right cultural capital to be in the social class to which they aspire.

These first two generations of the organization express disdain for the third generation of Basij youth not only because they represent a lower class but also because they see them as self-interested—they join to scale the social ladder. Mr. Ahmadi explained to me, "Those who went to the war went to fight for and defend the country, not to get better jobs or get into university, like the Basij of today. When you became a Basiji back then, you knew you could die at the warfront. You went because you really believed. But not today. Today these kids are opportunistic." There seemed to be some truth in the accusation of opportunism: several third-generation Basij filmmakers told me that they had joined because they did not have access to expensive filmmaking equipment. Once in the Basij, they could freely use such equipment to make their first films, a valuable stepping-stone.

I frequently heard the first two generations of Basijis say about the third generation, "They don't know exactly what they stand for." This was code for "They will stand for anything as long as it gets them ahead." "For us, it was a matter of life or death. These kids are just ideological and they don't even know why," Masoud, a war veteran and professional photographer who did freelance gigs for the cultural events of the Revolutionary Guard, whispered to me one day while we were in Abadan, the border town ninety miles from Basra, in southern Iraq, where the eight-year Iran-Iraq War started. There was a young intelligence minder from Tehran who had flown down "on assignment" from his pro-regime cultural organization to observe, report back, and control the cultural festival we were attending. He was there to make sure everything was "correct" for the cultural festival. He looked on with suspicion as the crew set up one of the theaters in Abadan. Masoud turned his back to the intelligence minder and his Abadani Basij counterparts and continued, "They don't even understand theater and film well enough to comment more than two sentences. But look at how arrogantly they stand there, posturing, trying to intimidate everyone. They wouldn't last a minute in the trenches in Abadan if Iraq invaded again right now." The first and second generations see "the kids" who joined the Basij, as they call them, as uncultured, incapable, blindly ideological, and uncouth. Younger Basijis, however, feel that the revolution has gone astray because the older generation has lost touch with its values. The revolution had offered Mostafa and his cohort a social mobility to which they saw the corruption of the older generation of revolutionaries as a threat. "They're the ones who are soft, not us," Ali, a Basiji of the third generation, told me. "We appreciate their sacrifices during the war, but they've become corrupted by money and obsessed with making themselves like the secular elite."

Parenting and Generational Differences in Postwar Iran

These generational differences were vast and significant. I found that the main factor that differentiated the first and second generation of the Basij from the third generation is the narrative of parenting, especially the challenges their children have posed to them. First- and second-generation Basijis who have become fathers often talked to me about listening to their children, mostly in their teens and early twenties, challenge their political, social, and cultural views. Those who have daughters, especially, talked to me extensively about how they began to question the stricter views they once held about the place of women in society, as their daughters now face restrictions. These men now understand the struggles of women in Iran in a more intimate fashion than their peers who do not have daughters, they explained. Almost all of them talked incessantly about their daughters' achievements and how much they resented the societal restrictions on women in Iran. They lamented the fact that they had supported a system that restricted women's advancement in society in the first decade of the revolution. They recalled that at the beginning of the Islamic Republic these restrictive policies were abstract for them. But today their daughters run up against these restrictions, and they now see the real-life consequences of their prior political actions.

"My daughters graduated at the top of their university classes," Yousef, a Basiji turned Revolutionary Guard, told me.

> One was in law school and the other is a chemical engineer. The lawyer comes home upset every day about how unfair it is that she can't become a judge but her lesser-qualified male classmates can. And you know what? She's perfectly right. We didn't fully understand what these restrictions would mean when we fought for them after the revolution. My daughters have helped me grow on these fronts. And because of that, I want our system to grow and make room for her, not turn her away in frustration.

Viewing the country through the eyes of a parent has changed the outlook of many in the first and second generation of Basijis. Ahmad, who has one teenage son and another in his early twenties, said to me:

> As my boys have grown, I've become less ideological. I'm still a political person, but I'm not passionate and fiery like I used to be thirty years ago. Now I constantly think about the kind of country my sons will live in. It's not just about

ideology anymore. It's about leaving my sons with a country they can comfortably prosper in. We don't need to put so many social restrictions on them.

In these narratives of parenting, children stand in for the future and stability. The first and second generations often attribute the more hard-line (*tond-ro*) tendencies of the third generation of Basijis to the fact that they don't yet have children. "These young kids [the third generation] do not yet instinctively think about what kind of system they wish to bequeath their children. This makes a difference in their outlook for the future of the state," the first and second generation often argued to me.

Once third-generation Basijis began to have children, I saw similar shifts. Toward the end of my fieldwork, five of my interlocutors in the third generation had babies. Thinking about their children's future led them to hope for stability. Reza, a twenty-eight-year-old Basiji who used to be the head of his university's Basij in Tehran and had suppressed protestors in 2009, said to me when his daughter was eight months old, "I used to welcome confrontation with the West so that they would stop bossing us around. But now when I hear my friends saying the same things I said only a year ago, I find myself automatically thinking of my daughter and wanting nothing but a peaceful country for her to grow up in."

2

Cracks in the Official Story

NEARLY ONE MONTH AFTER MR. AHMADI and some of his colleagues had been pushed out of the Center for the Chronicles of Victory, Mr. Hosseini invited Mr. Ahmadi to his office. I had spent the morning with Mr. Hosseini at an official event organized by the Supreme Leader's Office to celebrate the publication of new books on prisoners of war during the Iran-Iraq War.[1] Needing a break from the official pageantry of the event we had just attended, Mr. Hosseini decided to order chicken kabob and called Mr. Ahmadi to join us at his office. "We need to keep his spirits lifted. He's still upset over being ousted from the center," Mr. Hosseini said as he walked around the table in his office, setting out plates for lunch. The plastic to-go containers steamed on the table as we waited for Mr. Ahmadi.

Halfway through lunch, despite Mr. Hosseini's best attempts to keep the conversation light, Mr. Ahmadi pushed his plate of food away and folded his hands. "We created the culture that these young guys pretend to defend today. They think we're a threat to the very culture *we* created! They are such a joke. They think they're more ideological than us. *We* created this culture they're professing so much loyalty to!"

"Don't think about it anymore . . . "

" . . . I can't, Reza. They're sitting there in our offices now, and I'm here eating kabob with you."

"What's wrong with the kabob I gave you?" Mr. Hosseini protested, and they both began laughing. "Stop now with this talk. Let's get some chai in here. . . . Asghar Agha! Come bring us some chai please," Mr. Hosseini called out toward the hallway, "and come clear these plates. Mr. Ahmadi didn't like my kabob."

"Ey baba!" Mr. Ahmadi responded, laughing.

After Asghar Agha, an assistant at the center, cleared the table and brought us the tea and sweets, Mr. Ahmadi started again. "Reza, these kids don't even know that we edited all our films to match the message of the war. Our own propaganda has come back to literally kick us in the butt!"

"Yes, these kids don't understand the editing process. It's our own fault we didn't sit them down and tell them, 'Not all mothers wanted to send their sons to the war. We edited those scenes out!'"

"We didn't need to tell them," Mr. Ahmadi protested. "All they needed to do was read Avini himself. He said it in so many of his interviews."

"Bah! You think these kids read? I call this generation the sandwich generation. If we don't feed them information in little sandwich-bite pieces, they won't take any of it in. They don't read!"

"They took the propaganda of the war and believed it with all their hearts. And they didn't understand we needed to *create* that narrative because we were at war," Mr. Ahmadi said. "And now they fired me because I'm not *loyal enough* to the revolution! We created the revolution!" he claimed in exasperation, shaking his head and putting his forehead in his hands. "What do they think about the Imam's [Khomeini's] family supporting the Green Movement? Does the Imam's family not understand the revolution either? Ha!"

"That's what we're dealing with today, Mohammad," Mr. Hosseini said to his friend. "And we have to figure out a way to come to terms with them because, like it or not, they're the future of our system."

Internalizing the Official Story

In 2010 and 2011, I had traveled with a group of veterans to southern Iran along the Iran-Iraq border during the filming of my documentary. They were showing me the old battlefields they had fought on and recounting their stories. "To the left is where I was exposed to chemical gases," Ali C.

said, pointing to the endless expanse of dirt. No matter how many times I visited the battlefields in the south of the country, what struck me each time was how utterly barren they were; there was nowhere to hide or find shelter. As much as I read and studied the ins and outs of the war, there was nothing like visiting the battlefields with the veterans. As they pointed out where they had been injured, the vast, empty landscape spoke to the tragic reality of this war, with its trench warfare and its close combat.

"If you want, you can film me there telling my story," Ali said, interrupting my thoughts. Although my film was not about him, he had expressed interest in being filmed throughout our trip. I walked with him, leaving the group behind. There were some tanks in the background to the right, in an area that served as a museum of sorts to teach school children about the war. I asked Ali to stand on the other hill, away from the staged tanks, but he disagreed. "Ms. Bajoghli, I think it'd be better if you have the tanks behind me in the frame. And let me put this mask on my face so it's obvious that I'm a survivor of chemicals."

Because Ali never wore a mask, I told him he did not have to do so now. I also tried to change his mind on the location for his interview, but all to no avail. Ali, like most veterans, had been filmed numerous times by state television and was well versed in the aesthetics of state-produced war films. Since my film was about another veteran, I gave into Ali's wishes to be filmed as he thought fit. He donned a mask, asked me if I was ready with the camera, and when I pressed Record, he started: "In the name of God, the most merciful . . ."

I had already interviewed Ali off-camera many times over a span of four years for an oral history project on survivors of chemical warfare. In the beginning, he spoke to me very formulaically about his experiences at the front, just as he started to do in this staged video interview. By the third year, however, and much like the other war veterans I came to know throughout the years, Ali had let go of the official war rhetoric and opened up, offering his own narrative of his experiences. Ali spoke more openly regarding his doubts about the war, about his mistreatment by the government's Martyrs Foundation (Bonyād-e Shahid), and about his fears during the war itself.

The Martyrs Foundation is the official organization in the country in charge of veterans' affairs. Through a complicated system in which war disabilities are assigned percentages, the foundation gives veterans and their families medical coverage and aid. The higher a veteran's disability percentage, the higher the aid from the Martyrs Foundation. The foundation also provides low-interest home loans to veterans and their families. Although the foundation is a government entity that receives its funding from the national budget, it is also heavily involved in multimillion-dollar investment and infrastructure projects in the country, making it one of the most powerful foundations in Iran.[2]

By spending time with veterans in different settings, I learned under what circumstances veterans felt they could air their critical narratives and under what circumstances they felt they had to censor themselves. But the presence of my camera brought out an entirely different vocabulary. As soon as I turned it on, Ali code-switched to "official speak" and slipped into the rhetoric and comportment that the Islamic Republic's state television expected of him. The war veterans consciously distinguished between "the official" (*rasmi*) version and "the real" (*vāq'-ey*) version of the war. Their responses to state television crews about the war were formulaic and nearly identical, while their discussions among themselves and those whom they trusted took on an entirely different tone.

The consistent formula of the veterans' responses was not coincidental. The official narrative has continued on national television in Iran, and film crews from the Islamic Republic of Iran Broadcasting services coach veterans on the "right" way to speak about the war when they record them for the yearly war anniversary commemorations. As one veteran, Mohammad, said to me, "It's all theater. We don't believe a word that we have to say to them, but what can we do? We just have to play the role when they come." Ali had enacted the correct performance asked of him by state television crews when I turned on my camera. Off-camera, he recalled the war as "horrible," and he stated that he would "never want to go back to that time."

The state television crews also recognized the ways in which they as filmmakers also act as if they believe in the official story.[3] I was present when one state television film crew from a central province interviewed some veterans. When the director and cinematographer later invited me to join them for tea at a nearby cafeteria, they asked me what I thought about their pieces. I truthfully told them that the pieces they produced did not correspond with what I had learned from the veterans throughout my work. They agreed, and the director said, "But you know our hands are tied, Ms. Bajoghli." And then he asked for my address so that he could send me his "real" film work—work that was not dictated by state television. "Don't judge me by what you saw me doing today," he quietly pleaded. "I have a family to support and state television pays well. But I'll send you the work I really believe in to your personal address. Just don't share it with any of these guys," nodding toward the directors of two of the regime centers. Unbeknownst to the film director, those two regime center directors had also complained to me about having their hands tied, unable to choose how to represent the war in their programming.

These kinds of interactions were common as I got to know the filmmakers behind official state media. When their producers left the room, they often connected the personal hard drives that they kept in their briefcases to show me the work they actually cared about. Oftentimes, they showed me short art films with themes of love and belonging. They eagerly sent these films out to film festivals, which could give them the cultural capital they desired and the ability to one day be independent filmmakers who did not rely on paychecks from state television. They also shared with me the videos and audio recordings they had found of interviews, lectures, and behind-the-scenes footage from internationally recognized *gheyr-e khodi* ("other," or outsider) directors, such as Asghar Farhadi and Abbas Kiarostami. They studied these clips closely and tried to apply the lessons in their work. But I observed that at work they carefully hid their ambitions for their film projects. When I asked why, the answers were similar: "The work we do for television is good money. That's how we support our families," Mansour, thirty years old, said to me. "We're not like the independent filmmakers [*filmsāz-hā-ye mostaqel*], you see," added Hadi, twenty-eight years old. "Those kids [independent filmmakers] are rich. They can afford not to work for money for some time. We need a salary to pay our rent and take care of our kids. If I had their circumstances, I wouldn't be here making these pieces for state television." It is not that they did not believe in making media for the regime, but rather that the restrictions state television placed on them meant that they had to make media they found to be "dry" and "boring," as they often remarked.

Landing a job in a regime production studio or cultural center—which provides a middle-class living for filmmakers, photographers, and writers—involves being a *khodi* (insider). First, the potential employee must come recommended by either someone who already works at the cultural center or production studio and has the proper revolutionary credentials and a track record of public piety, or he must be someone whom the director of the center trusts. Crucially, the candidate must be vouched for by someone who is "trustworthy," meaning a pious employee of the government or a cultural center. Only after this recommendation does the candidate go through an interview process at the cultural center. At this stage, he is asked about his work experience and portfolio. But more importantly, he is interviewed about his religious knowledge. If he passes this round, the cultural center investigates his family to ensure it is religious enough and politically loyal. "The most important criteria is who recommended the candidate and how religious he is," the director of one of the main regime cultural centers said when I asked him how a new hire got the job.

When full-time employment is not available at a cultural center or in a production studio, young regime filmmakers can be hired as freelance contractors, much like media workers in other countries. These tend to be long-term gigs, always acquired through an insider connection and usually with one of the channels of the state television service. A number of third-generation Basijis who were my interlocutors made their living in this way. They were hired as contractors for the Qur'an Channel, for example, or Channel 3 and worked on specific shows or segments. The vast majority did not like their jobs at the state television service because of its "dry atmosphere," as they repeatedly told me, and because of how much they had to censor their work. But it paid well, enough to support their families, and it also allowed them access to the best camera and editing equipment. Some then managed to use this equipment on their personal films.

The Real versus the Official

Veterans differentiate their stories from the official state narratives. The official war culture—created by state cultural centers, broadcast on national television, depicted on large murals, mapped onto street names, and housed in museums—is repetitive and "boring," as veterans often voiced to me. The same story of pious individuals willing to martyr themselves for the good of the Islamic Republic is told over and over again via these different media. There is no novelty to these stories. The official narrative of the war has stayed the same throughout the past three decades. On the other hand, the real stories are characterized by secrecy, revelation, novelty, and anger. As Ali's story above illustrates, he can let his guard down and tell his story only in the company of those whom he trusts. As soon as there is any potential of the story being made public (i.e., via the camera), he switches to the official story. Every real story of the war that I heard from veterans happened in these private ways. When they determined it was safe enough, they began to tell me their stories in hushed voices.

War veterans in Iran hold a prized place in society not only as veterans but also as guardians of the revolution. Because the war came on the heels of the revolution and because many of the men who fought did so as volunteers, they are regarded not only as soldiers but also as the protectors of the revolution. Within the political lore of the Islamic Republic, the Basijis and members of the Revolutionary Guard who fought in the war hold pride of place in the protection and advancement of the Islamic Republic. As guardians of the revolution, they have much more leeway to criticize the state or politicians than do nonveterans in Iran, but even those who volunteered to fight and continue to support the idea of the Islamic Republic are not immune from reprisal. Thus, they continue to conceal their "real" stories or only choose to tell them when the circumstances are right.

One case in particular drew a great deal of media attention and resulted in a heated debate in the country about the hypocrisy of turning veterans into symbolic heroes but not actually caring for them. The case was presented in the documentary film *Haj Kazem* (dir. Masoud Najafi, 2013). The film follows the actor Parviz Parastui as he attempts to get medical care for Nasser Afshari, a veteran who suffers from exposure to chemical weapons. Parastui is a famous actor who made his name by acting in powerful films about the war, as well as in films that criticize the clerical establishment. The documentary *Haj Kazem* echoes one of Parastui's best-known films, the fictional *Agence Shishei* (*The Glass Agency*, dir. Ebrahim Hatamikia, 1998), in which his character, Haj Kazem, attempts to help his former commander in the war leave Iran for medical help. When he is unsuccessful and, moreover, feels that he and his commander have been disrespected because they are veterans, Haj Kazem takes hostages in a travel agency. The film's honest (though fictional) portrayal of the desperation that many veterans feel in attempting to get the care they need made Parastui a celebrity among veterans. And because his own brother was killed during the war, Parastui has made it a personal mission to champion the care of veterans in the country.

In the documentary *Haj Kazem* (named after the character in *The Glass Agency*), Parastui becomes a real-life Haj Kazem, trying to take Afshari abroad for the care that he needs. The film intercuts Afshari's case with scenes from *The Glass Agency*, with a younger Parastui enacting the same story in the fictional setting. The documentary draws out the sense of absurdity that Parastui feels when his life begins to imitate his art from fifteen years before.

The Martyrs Foundation under the Ahmadinejad administration began to deny coverage for treatment that severely wounded veterans received in Europe, insisting that they continue their care in Iran instead. Prior to this ban, Afshari had traveled to Germany every few months to receive specialized care, which cost the Martyrs Foundation 15 million toman (USD 12,000 at the time). After Afshari's endless petitions to the foundation and the president's office fell on deaf ears and he began to feel sicker and sicker, he enlisted the help of Parastui.

One of their first efforts to draw attention to Afshari's case included a staged conversation between Parastui and Afshari. That conversation and the foundation's refusal to send him abroad were covered in all the major newspapers of the country due to Parastui's celebrity. Without Parastui, Afshari's case would have been pushed aside, as most veterans' cases are, Afshari tells the camera. Journalists and online commentators heavily criticized the Martyrs Foundation for refusing care while its coffers were full. The public pressure on the foundation became so great that state television, usually silent on such topics, was forced to cover the story. In the state television interview, Parastui and Afshari heavily criticized the foundation for its hypocrisy in treating veterans, an act that would have been near impossible for Afshari without Parastui's star power.

The Martyrs Foundation is one of the wealthiest private foundations in the country; as a result, it draws ire not only from veterans but also from the general public. In the film, Parastui says to the camera, "Is this right? We spend so much money on everything else in this country and we've all benefited from the war. We can't send these wounded veterans to get treatment?" He continues, "We created the Martyrs Foundation to be in the service of the war. So that means they're supposed to serve the veterans. They are not supposed to be there to make themselves personally rich."

Haj Kazem shows the length (and years) that someone of Parastui's stature had to go to in order to get Afshari the care he needed in Germany. In the end, despite the fact that President Ahmadinejad bowed to public pressure and asked the foundation to tend to Afshari's case, the foundation did not budge. Finally, Parastui was able to raise donations from the public to get Afshari to Germany. When Afshari arrived in Germany, his physicians told him that if his treatment had been delayed just a few more months, he would have died.

The Creation of Official Stories

The creation of a war culture to normalize the conflict and to militarize the cultural field is not exclusive to Iran.[4] In the twentieth century, states have developed war cultures to support their respective war efforts. The Iranian case in the 1980s is no different. Officially called *farhang-e defâ'e moghadas*, "the culture of the sacred defense" was developed to support the eight-year Iran-Iraq War. This war culture was all-consuming. As written about extensively elsewhere, war culture in Iran developed in films, literature, and photography through a plethora of state-sponsored organizations.[5] But, crucially, production of the war culture did not end when the ceasefire was signed in 1988. Instead, as I argue throughout the book, this war culture continued to develop and expand in postwar Iran, precisely because the war is the foundational narrative of the Islamic Republic.

The war film industry and the many institutions created to support it began to emerge shortly after Iraq invaded Iran. At the beginning of the war, the War Group Team at Islamic Republic of Iran Broadcasting produced television documentaries about the war and, shortly thereafter, the Ministry of Culture and Islamic Guidance created the War Films Bureau at the Farabi

Cinema Foundation with the task of depicting the "sacred defense" as a spiritual question. The creation of this official narrative began at the outset of the war. During the war's eight years, fifty-six feature films of the war film genre were produced in Iran, and most of these focused on military operations. Of all genres in postrevolutionary Iranian cinema, war films have been the most consistently used means of delivering state-approved messages about Islamic and revolutionary values.

The most significant contributor to Iran's filmic war culture came from the powerful representations of the war in Morteza Avini's documentaries. Avini's influential series *Chronicles of Victory* (*Revāyat-e Fath*) was shot on the front lines and broadcast weekly on national television. With only two channels on state television at that time, the *Chronicles of Victory* series served to create an imagined community par excellence. This series brought footage from the front lines to the homes of millions of Iranians across the country and gave them their first glimpses of the war. More importantly, it urged young male viewers to join the war. The voice-over narration that Avini employed throughout the series was heavy on the religious and spiritual causes that led Iranian soldiers to fight against enemy attackers. "You'd need a Shi'a dictionary to understand Avini's narration today," Mr. Hosseini said to me. "It was a narration that belonged to that time, but it's not understandable today."

Avini's films presented the war as the setting where men emulated Imam Hussain, the grandson of the Prophet Mohammad and the third Shi'a Imam, who refused to pledge allegiance to Yazid and was martyred, along with his seventy-two companions, by Yazid's army in Karbala in 680 AD. The day of his death continues to be commemorated in Shi'a communities as an event in which the Prophet's grandson refused to bow to an authority he deemed as oppressive to him and his kin. During the Iran-Iraq War, Iranian politicians and cultural producers used Imam Hussain to symbolize their position vis-à-vis the invading Iraqi army. Iranian soldiers were likened to Imam Hussain and his companions. The battlefront was thus framed as a pious space and the soldiers lauded as ideal citizens. Avini's documentary series on state television was arguably the most influential mass production that propagated this narrative during the war.

Avini's films were made specifically to serve the war effort, with the primary goal of recruiting more young men to fight. Avini explicitly stated in his writings and interviews that he deleted scenes that did not communicate his version of the "truth" of the war, according to which Iranians were completely loyal to Ayatollah Khomeini and soldiers were ready to die for the revolution. In one interview, Avini asked, "If the camera focused on a mother and she spoke with a bad tone saying: 'I don't want my child to go to war,' what should we do with this in the editing process? Should we delete these scenes or keep them?" Avini responded honestly to his own question, "We would never leave such a scene in our film, because this scene does not correspond with the truth of our society."[6] The censorship of critical voices was a key facet of Avini's documentaries during the war.

Once the war ended, a conscious decision was made to transform the war from a military confrontation with Iraq to a cultural and social confrontation in Iranian cities and towns. In addition to the cultural and moral policing that took place, as discussed in chapter 1, regime cultural producers continued to use the battlefront as a trope in which issues of proper citizenship and revolutionary identity played out. In this effort, Avini founded the Narrative Foundation (Bonyad-e Revāyat). The Narrative Foundation's main goal was to continue producing films in service of the war culture, with a specific focus on transmitting the spirit of the battlefront and communicating the lessons learned during the war. The Narrative Foundation also serves as an umbrella for a variety of cultural centers in Iran, all devoted to producing cultural material related to the values of the war. This foundation and the centers under it receive further funding and political clout from the Revolutionary Guard and Basij. These centers include the following:

the Center for the Cinematic Arts of the Revolution and Sacred Defense (Markaz-e Anjoman-e Honar-hā-e Cinemā-ye Enghelāb va Defāe Moghadas);

the Cinema Center of the Revolution and Sacred Defense (Markaz Anjoman Cinemā-ye Enghelāb va Defāe Moghadas);

the Theater Association of the Revolution and Sacred Defense (Anjoman-e Teatr-e Enghelāb va Defāe Moghadas);

the Center for the Chronicles of Victory of the Revolution and Sacred Defense, which houses the archive of Avini's film crew; and

the Cinematic Association of the Revolution and the Sacred Defense
(Anjoman-e Cinemā-ye Enghelāb va Defāe Moghadas), which funds a large
production studio, the City of the Sacred Defense Cinema.

War films are filmed at the City of the Sacred Defense Cinema, as well as
popular television series about historical periods. This space, off the highway
between Tehran and Qom, is also funded and guarded by the Revolutionary
Guard and Basij because it holds weaponry from the Iran-Iraq War.

Overarching these centers is the Howzeh Honari. It is the most important
regime cultural center in the country. Founded at the beginning of the 1979
Revolution, it was placed under the umbrella of the Organization for Islamic
Propagation (OIP; *sāzmān-e tablighāt-e islāmi*), the country's most promi-
nent organization for the promotion of the regime. Howzeh Honari is the
OIP's largest center and receives financial and political support from the Sup-
reme Leader's Office. Located in central Tehran on Hafez Street, near the old
American Embassy, the Howzeh Honari is housed in a beautiful former Baha'i
cultural center that the new government commandeered following the 1979
Revolution.

It is also the most securitized regime cultural center I entered in Tehran,
besides the media center attached to the Martyrs Foundation. The gate of the
center has two security offices, one for men and the other for women. The
women's section is arguably harder to get through, as the guard not only asks
the woman trying to enter who she is there to see but also checks if her hijab
and clothing are acceptable. Although I visited this center countless times
throughout my research, there was never a time when I was not stopped by
(usually the same) female guard and asked to fix my veil, lower my overcoat
sleeves, not wear jeans the next time I came—the list of complaints about my
dress and presence as a woman seemed endless. It was also the only center
where, even though I had the support of the director of the cultural center as
well as some of their filmmakers, the instructors of the filmmaking unit denied my requests to sit in on filmmaking classes for research purposes because my hijab did not meet their standards. When I offered to wear more
conservative clothing (even though my hijab and clothing were always conservative when I was conducting research), the main instructor denied my
requests again. "Bad hijab" is an easy and oft-used foil to deny women access
to places. When one of the filmmakers of the center called the instructor on

my behalf and asked what I needed to do in order to get access, the main instructor said, "There's nothing she can do. I refuse to allow her in my classes because she's not one of us."

The Package

I was about to leave Iran for a few months. On the day before my flight, I got a text message from Mr. Ahmadi: "I know it's your last day and you must be busy. But meet me at the office if you can. We have something to give you."

Two hours later, I took the subway downtown to his office near Palestine Square. Mr. Ahmadi waited for me in the lobby in his wheelchair. He had a big smile on his face. "You haven't gotten rid of us yet," he joked. He led me to his office and closed the door behind him, a motion that caught my attention since he always left the door open when we met. In his office were two other men, Ali and Hasan, both war veterans and close friends of Mr. Ahmadi, and I had seen them many times in his office.

"We don't want to keep you too long," Mr. Ahmadi said as he pulled out a small package from a drawer in his desk. "This is for you. But you have to promise us you won't open it until you're out of Iran."

"Put it at the bottom of your suitcase," Ali said, "and make sure they don't make you open it at the airport here."

"It's a film that you need to see. And when you're back, we'll discuss it," Mr. Ahmadi said. Mr. Ahmadi handed me a VCD that he had bound in multiple envelopes and then wrapped in bubble wrap with three rounds of tape on top. It was the most secure thing I ever took out of Iran.

When I arrived in New York, I opened the carefully wrapped package. On the VCD, Mr. Ahmadi had written in red permanent ink: *Marsie-e Barā-ye āshegh*, 1382, Kārgardān: Ahmad Soleimania (*An Elegy for the Loved*, 2003, Director: Ahmad Soleimania). I put it in my computer and waited for it to load.

A documentary set inside the Sadr Psychiatric Hospital and the Saadatabad Psychiatric Wellness Center, the film harshly criticizes the regime for its care of veterans. With much voice-over narration throughout the film, the camera pans the hospital as the narrator explains that many of the veterans suffer from post-traumatic stress disorder and other mental health illnesses due to what they witnessed on the battlefront. The film cuts to footage from the war, showing the shattered body of a soldier, torn apart by a bomb. The narrator continues, "Many of them have depression, anxiety . . . They cannot sit still . . . They feel like they're being choked . . . They have shortness of breath."

The film then cuts to a patient in the hospital who is shaking uncontrollably. He looks at the director and says, "I have nothing to say. I have nothing" (*Sohbati nadāram. Hichi nadāram*).

Another veteran speaks directly to the camera: "I have nothing to say. I can't remember anything. I have forgetfulness [*farāmushi*]. . . . I've been electrocuted too much. I can't remember anything. They give me something so I'll pass out, then send shocks through me so my body jerks, and when they're done, my eyes are bloodred, like I'm bleeding." Then the camera returns to the shaking veteran: "I don't remember anything because of the shocks I've received."

A wife looks straight into the camera and starts to speak. Her husband yells at her from the background to stop. She doesn't listen. "Anytime someone tries to speak the truth, they say that person is crazy. The war is over! These people went to fight for us!" she says, raising her voice.

The camera then pans to show the unkempt conditions and lack of resources in the hospital. The film cuts to close-ups of the patients who all look like they have been heavily medicated and undergone electroshock therapy. Sons, daughters, wives, and other patients talk to the camera, discussing their despair. One wife says of her husband, who lies in bed, "I've been told to put him in a home, but I can't bring myself to do that. The Bonyād [Martyrs Foundation] has deemed him 25 percent injured, so we can't even get proper care for him. Does he look 25 percent injured to you?" Her husband can no longer speak and communicates by blinking his eyes.

The film goes on like this, with no traditional narrative arc. Instead, it is a series of interviews intercut with images from the conditions of the hospital. In the parts of the film with the harshest criticism of the regime, loud music drowns out the words of the protestors. I later learned that the filmmaker made this decision hoping to be able to air the film on national television. Despite this precaution, state television refused to air the film.

When I returned to Iran months later, I texted Mr. Ahmadi to ask if we could get together to discuss what he had given me. He invited me to his office after work a few days later. He told me that the director had made this film in 2003, and nearly ten years later it was still making the rounds among veterans. The director had attempted multiple times to have the film aired on national television, but even though the filmmaker's other work has been on national television, this film was turned down because of its critical content. That's when the director decided to distribute the film to veterans via VCDs and Bluetooth. He wanted to show them how the state treats their colleagues in the mental hospitals.

Some veterans have held informal viewing parties at their homes with their families. During these informal screenings, they often angrily charge that they have been "used" by the state and then forgotten. "I couldn't stop crying when I saw this film," Mr. Ahmadi told me. "I made my kids see it too so they understood how dirty politics is. How all they hear about the war is fake. The politicians actually don't care about us. They would prefer if we would all disappear in institutions like you see in this film, and they'll throw the keys away."

For Mr. Ahmadi, sitting there in his wheelchair, this film and the regime's mistreatment of the veterans hit close to home. He continued, "You saw how they really treat veterans. You saw how all these politicians have gotten rich off our sacrifices, while they continue to tell lies about the war and treat us like animals."

The film holds power precisely because it tells a story very much at odds with the official narrative, which ironically, Mr. Ahmadi had a large role in creating, before he was ousted by the younger generation of regime media makers.

3

Insiders, Outsiders, and Belonging

ON A COLD WINTER AFTERNOON in January 2014 in Tehran, I received a call from Mr. Hosseini: "Ms. Bajoghli, come to a private meeting tonight at 6:00 p.m. in Sureh Publishing House. You don't want to miss this." Already struggling from a headache due to the day's unbearable pollution, I found a heavy-duty mask in my apartment before heading out. Ever since sanctions against Iran had increased over its nuclear issue, Tehran's chronic pollution had worsened. I futilely hoped the mask would guard against the pollutants. I made my way out onto the city's hazy streets clogged with rush-hour traffic.

Though the ride should have taken only fifteen minutes, I arrived at Sureh, the Howzeh Honari's publishing house, located in the center of the city, an hour later. Sureh is responsible for producing literature on the Iran-Iraq War. In the complex political world of publishing in the Islamic Republic, Sureh fares extremely well, receiving government subsidies for high-quality paper and permission to publish as it pleases. It was a strategic place for the meeting that was about to take place.[1]

I saw Mr. Hosseini in the doorway with his briefcase in hand and an excited look on his face. He rushed me downstairs to the meeting room. We were the first ones there, and he wanted to give me an idea of what was going to happen before everyone arrived. "I've gathered what you could call the Islamic Ku Klux Klan," he said to me laughing. "These are the most hard-line people you are going to meet, but you'll see how I'll turn them around by the end of tonight."

He explained to me that a few days earlier he had attended the funeral of the father of Iran's most famous feminist filmmaker. After the ceremony, an emerging filmmaker, Mohsen Amir-Youssefi, approached him and asked for help. Amir-Youssefi, who won the Camera d'Or Special Mention at the 2004 Cannes Film Festival for his film *Bitter Dream* (*Khāb-e Talkh*), is one of the new generation of independent Iranian filmmakers who have been mentored by Iran's famous international film directors Abbas Kiarostami, Jafar Panahi, and Asghar Farhadi—all considered *gheyr-e khodi* (outsider) from the point of view of regime cultural producers. Amir-Youssefi had just finished a new film that was set during the emergence of the Green Movement in 2009. The Fajr Film Festival, Iran's largest and most prestigious international film festival, had refused to screen the film after initially accepting it.

"The hard-liners want to go after this film, and ultimately that's going to be bad for us," Mr. Hosseini told me. In this instance, "us" meant the regime. As I had gotten to know Mr. Hosseini through the years, I came to realize he cleverly negotiated among the various roles he inhabited: though a captain of the Revolutionary Guard, a former Basij, and an eight-year veteran of the war, he had also gotten his PhD in literature after the war, boasted of having friends of all political stripes, and had helped in getting gheyr-e khodi artists out of prison after they had been arrested during the Green Movement. That day at Sureh, Mr. Hosseini wore a fully buttoned-up shirt, and despite the heat in the building, his sleeves were not pulled up. Although usually clean-shaven, he sported a very faint beard for meetings like this one. In short, for the purposes of the meeting, Mr. Hosseini was visibly pro-regime.

He rushed to tell me why we were there, before his guests arrived: "Mohsen [Amir-Youssefi] wanted me to help get his film approved for Fajr, and I thought the best thing I could do is invite the cultural critics of the most conservative papers to watch the film and have a dialogue with the filmmaker." The writers invited that afternoon were from *Kayhan*, Tasnim, *RajaNews*, and Fars News Agency, as well as key university leaders from Ansar-e Hezbollah and the Basij.[2] As Mr. Hosseini immediately revealed, this kind of meeting, where writers from Iran's most hard-line publications sat face to face with a gheyr-e khodi filmmaker like Amir-Youssefi, had never happened before.

As the journalists and Basij student leaders, including Mostafa, all men in their twenties, walked into the room, Mr. Hosseini stood next to me and introduced them one by one. In all of our interactions together throughout the years, Mr. Hosseini had a clear strategy when introducing me to others. When he deemed it appropriate, he would let me navigate the terrain on my own. But in instances such as this one, where the men I was to meet represented the most hard-line factions in the country, Mr. Hosseini would position himself beside me in order to show them his trust and validation of my presence at the meeting. Without a person like Mr. Hosseini to make this sort of endorsement on my behalf, I would not have been welcomed in such a pro-regime space. Mr. Hosseini's proximity made the journalists smile back at me, put their hands respectfully on their hearts, and bow slightly as they said hello to me from across the room.[3]

We sat in Sureh's cinema room, set up with theater seating. I positioned myself at the back corner of the room so that I could have a view of everything, but also because as a woman in a conservative political setting, I was expected to sit in the back. A few months earlier, at an event for former prisoners of war organized by a branch of the Supreme Leader's Office, I had taken a seat in the front row and was kindly asked by a young man before the event started if I could move back a few rows. When I got up to move, I saw some of the women looking at me scornfully and a few of the younger men waiting for me to move so that one could take my place.

In my haste to leave my apartment that afternoon so I would make it to the meeting on time, I had forgotten to wear a thinner overcoat under my puffy down winter coat, as is the norm in winter in Iran, so that when indoors, I could take the winter coat off and still be "properly" dressed. As usual, the heater was turned up in the room and it felt like an uncomfortable eighty degrees. In most other public settings, I would have taken off my coat and left it draped over my legs, but in this setting, I knew better. Sweating, I consigned myself to unzipping the coat just slightly, making sure my scarf covered my neck, and I willed my body to cool down.

As the journalists settled in the room, Mr. Hosseini welcomed them, "You guys represent all the conservative factions in the country. If someone bombs this place tonight, half the country will be relieved." They all laughed heartily at the joke.

Mr. Hosseini continued, "Our artists don't know much about what's right and what's wrong, and when they do something wrong and we criticize it, they then jump down our throats and say we censor them. And maybe this is our fault. I wanted you guys to come tonight because instead of making news against this film and making it more famous by banning it and writing critically about it, let's watch it together and decide if we can take a different approach."

With that, Mr. Hosseini pressed Play to start the film to be debated that night, *Āshghāl-hā-ye Dust-dāshtani* (*Desirable Garbage*). The title refers to Mahmoud Ahmadinejad calling the protestors of the Green Movement *khas-o khāshāk* (garbage). The director of the film turned Ahmadinejad's language on its head, signposting his politics before the first frame even came on screen.

Desirable Garbage starts in the throes of the Green Movement: protestors, running away from paramilitary forces on motorcycles. Seeking refuge, they stream into the yard of Monir, an old woman. Sima, Monir's sister-in-law, has led the protestors to Monir's yard, mentioning to the protestors with excitement that this moment feels like the 1979 protests that led to the fall of the Shah. Incredibly, for a film made in Iran, it depicts the paranoia of 2009. The noise of approaching motorcycles was terrifying, because the motorcycles likely bore Basijis who had come to attack any demonstrator in sight. The film depicts protestors marked with paint guns that the Basij and riot police used on running protestors whom they would later pick up on sweeps and take to prison.

The elderly Monir scolds her sister-in-law and says she wants all of the protestors out of her yard. She is beset by fear that her house will be targeted the next day by security forces. As she gets them out of the yard, Monir has flashbacks: Her husband had been in the administration of Prime Minister Mohammad Mossadegh, who had nationalized Iranian oil in 1950 and was ousted in a CIA-orchestrated coup in 1953. One of her sons had been killed fighting in the Iran-Iraq War. Another son had avoided the war and went abroad to study and stayed there. Her brother had been executed after the

revolution for being a leftist. And her sister-in-law, Sima, had been a revolutionary in 1979, but after the "cleansing" (*pāksāzi*) and the Islamization of the country, she had been forced to give up her dreams and become a housewife. Monir's
family encompasses the various narratives of Iran's contemporary history.

After Monir orders all the protestors out of her yard, she becomes anxious that the security forces will show up to her house in the morning and
question her about providing refuge for them. In a frenzy, she begins to
rid her house of anything that the security forces might find problematic
if they searched her home. Grabbing trash bags, she cleanses her house of
VHS tapes of old Iranian movies, her illegal satellite dish, and the family
albums from before the revolution in which the women are pictured without hijabs. As she's gathering things to throw away, she talks to her dead
husband's photo. She goes through his old stuff and disposes of his neckties,
their cassette tapes of prerevolutionary Iranian singers, and anything she
finds that refers to the time before the revolution. Her husband comes to
life in the framed picture and complains to Monir, "What you are doing is
erasing and killing our culture!"

"I have no choice," Monir responds to the frame, as if the framed dead
always awaken to keep her company. She continues cleansing and purging.
She goes into the room of Ramin, her son who is now abroad. Monir throws
away his posters of Kafka and his favorite Western bands. At this point, both
her sons come to life in their respective picture frames: Ramin, who wears
a graduation cap and gown, and Amir, in fatigues at the battlefront, before
he was killed. Amir says to his brother: "Aren't you ashamed that you left the
country when we were at war? Couldn't your studying wait?"

Monir pleads with them to stop fighting, and Amir agrees to help his
mother make decisions about their family pictures: which ones she should
throw away, which ones she should cut out certain people from, and which
ones she should edit with a marker to cover up her arms and hair. Amir tells
his mother to get rid of the framed photo of her brother Mansour, the leftist
activist executed in prison after the revolution. As Monir throws Mansour's
photo away, he comes to life in the frame, addressing his sister, "They're
even afraid of our pictures now! The thought of our memory terrifies them,"
referring to Amir and the supporters of the Islamic Republic. Monir's talking

photos attack each other, each blaming the other for the state of the country today. In a sense, their story is a story of fratricide (*famil-koshi*), and how Iranian families have had to *pāk-sāz* (cleanse) their lives constantly in order to survive in ever-changing and unpredictable political circumstances. Monir stays up all night sifting through her beloved objects, and as day dawns, she throws the incriminating ones in the trash.

As the film's credits rolled, there was a heavy silence in the room. With its overt references to the political executions in the prisons following the revolution and its depictions of the very real task that many Iranian families perform on a daily basis, hiding the "unrevolutionary" part of their lives in order to conform with the fact that they lead one life publicly and a different life privately, this was the most blatantly political film against the Islamic Republic that I had ever seen produced inside Iran.

The lights came back on, and the journalists and student leaders looked at each other with disgust. The director had yet to show up to the meeting, and they began to turn their ire on Mr. Hosseini.

"What the hell was this movie? How did the Ahmadinejad administration even give permission for this film to be made? I want to know your opinion, Mr. Hosseini!" Mostafa said. "Why even invite us to see this film? What is this horrible film doing? My heart hurts after watching it. What does this film want to accomplish anyway? There's no way we can even start to say what scenes the director needs to change to make it better."

Mr. Hosseini responded, "The intellectuals (*rowshanfekrs*) in our country are supported by outside forces [i.e., the Iranian diaspora and foreign powers]; they will make this film popular because of its content. Let's see what we can do to minimize the impact of this film."

The reporter from Fars News raised his hands angrily. Barely able to control his voice, he blurted out, "This is not just a political film! This is antirevolutionary!"

Mr. Hosseini attempted to calm them down. The more the conservative press writes against this film, the more the intellectuals and Iranian diaspora media will rally behind it, Mr. Hosseini argued. "Let's not contribute to making this film more popular by writing against it," he pleaded.

The director walked in at this point and apologized for being late, giving the usual excuse of being caught in Tehran's traffic. The journalists became quiet and stood up to respectfully greet him. They smiled and introduced themselves, as if they had not been excoriating him just seconds earlier. After exchanging pleasantries, Mr. Hosseini asked Amir-Youssefi to talk about the process of making the film.

A tall man in his early forties with broad shoulders, Amir-Youssefi launched into his story. "It took me one and a half years to get permission to make this film," he explained.

> Before we even began shooting, I had to do seven rewrites of the screenplay in order for the Ministry of Culture to approve the film. After all that, I received no funding. Eventually, after much back-and-forth, the Farabi Cinema Foundation offered funding, but I had to rewrite the script another eight times before we could start filming.[4] Farabi specifically asked for sixty-eight things to be changed and deleted, and we obeyed. After all of this, when the Fajr Festival told us it wouldn't show the film, we were very confused. When we got the news that the festival was refusing to screen our film, I told the festival directors that we didn't understand their refusal; even Fars News hadn't written against us!

The Fars News editor chimed in from the audience: "Well, we hadn't seen the film. Now that we have . . . " and he began to laugh.

Amir-Youssefi smiled nervously at the comment before he continued, "My goal is to try to show all sides of Iran and to demonstrate empathy (ham-dardi). There's no other film like this in Iran yet. I want people to see this from the mother's point of view: that she loves all of these conflicting sides, that they are all a part of her. I ask you all not to get caught up in the fights that the framed pictures have with each other. Instead, put yourself in the mother's place."

The Fars News editor addressed Amir-Youssefi. "I have nothing against you," he said.

> You are a director and you are doing your job. My strongest criticism for this film lies with the cultural administrators of our country who let this film even be made in the first place. But I want you to know, I think that

most films made about the *fetneh* [sedition, i.e., Green Movement] are done without any kind of research, just like your film. And when we write about this, then readers start to say, "Oh no, here come the cultural al-Qaeda again!" referring to us. But my question to you is, How can you make a film where you show people are scared when they hear the sound of motorcycles? How can you link 2009 with the 1979 Revolution and Mossadegh's coup? That's unfathomable! In my opinion, you intellectuals are very dictatorial. You've gotten money from the government to make your film and you make an anti-regime film! Why did you take government money and make this film? Why does your film show that people's houses and phones were bugged in 2009? Is that how it really was? You're being unfair! It's wrong that you think that a filmmaker can make whatever he wants, but we can't criticize you or the film!

The *RajaNews* journalist, a young man in his mid-twenties, nodded in agreement and jumped in, "We watch twenty films per year and feel like in every one the director has offended *our* core beliefs and values. The films that are made are all from your point of view!" The journalists in the room chimed in their agreement. The *RajaNews* journalist, his voice getting discernibly louder, continued,

Our biggest problem with you all is that for thirty-five years you have closed your eyes to us. You don't see us! We're so tired of you all depicting the Islamic Republic in such clichéd terms in your films. It's all just showing our boys saying, "Sister, fix your veil!" We're more complex than that. Don't offend us! If you want to offend the government, fine, but when you offend us, you're offending the people. If you're so concerned with the political executions after the revolution, go and read the real stories about these people and then you'll understand why we had to execute them!

The *RajaNews* journalist, red in the face, rose out of his seat, leaning forward toward the director, and just short of screaming, demanded, "If you want to make a film against the government, that's okay with us. But don't make a film against the regime!"

This journalist, like other regime cultural producers, made the distinction between the government (*dowlat*), which is made up of the president, the parliament, and the ministers, who can be voted in and out of office, and the regime (*nezām*), which embodies the framework of the Islamic Republic and the belief in the *velāyat-e faqih* (rule of jurisprudence). The government can come under criticism, but the regime, in the eyes of the regime cultural producers, cannot be challenged.

Amir-Youssefi, visibly sweating at this point, said in his own defense, "The leftists don't like my film either. I'm telling you this so you don't think that it's just you all who don't like it and don't agree with it." Amir-Youssefi turned to the *RajaNews* journalist directly and asked, "Why do you think your work is not important? Your work has a big effect on us. What you all write has a big effect on us and our films."

"More people watch your films than read our articles!" the *RajaNews* journalist responded. Despite their formal power, he declared that he and his colleagues ultimately feel ignored. He then expanded on his claims that insiders' stories are not told with the same dignity as the stories of outsiders: "Why not give two minutes in your film to the Basij or the security forces on the street? Why not see what he has to say?"

A self-identified Basiji journalist from the city of Isfahan added, "We've never seen our own people in films. I've never even seen my own generation in Iranian films: the third generation of Basiji and Hezbollahi. The only Basiji I ever see in films is the dead one on the battlefront. In this film, the Greens are terrified of us, but no one sees us. Who are we? Why don't you give us a voice in your film? Who are these Basijis and plainclothes men on the motorcycles with the batons you show in passing? Those plainclothes authorities are us! Give us a voice!" he demanded.

Amir-Youssefi shot back quickly, "I feel that your voice is always broadcast on television and in many films. But for me, those first few days of the Green Movement, for the first time in my life, I finally saw the people. I saw our society."

"You mean you've never been to a march (*rāhpeymāyi*) before?" the Fars News editor asked angrily, referring to the official pro-regime marches that take place on important holidays and for significant events, such as the Jerusalem Day celebrations or the anniversary of the taking of the U.S. Embassy.

Mr. Hosseini interrupted to calm down the journalists. The fact that Amir-Youssefi had referred to the protestors of the Green Movement as "the people" had hit a raw nerve for the Fars News editor and the others in the room, who scoffed at him.

Amir-Youssefi responded, "Every march that I'd seen prior to the big silent protest the day the election results were announced, I saw only people who looked like you all. But in the Green Movement, I saw a whole cross-section of the population that's never visible at the official marches."

When the Islamic Republic created laws about permissible dress following the 1979 Revolution, it politicized outward appearances to the point where Amir-Youssefi and the journalists could use them to demarcate khodi (insider) versus gheyr-e khodi (outsider). For Amir-Youssefi and others in his social circle, the government-decreed marches bring out only people who "looked like you all"—meaning men with facial hair, closed collars, and slacks and women with pious hijab: little to no makeup, hair completely covered, dressed mainly in black. In other words, the regime's khodis. In the Green Movement, Amir-Youssefi said he finally saw "the people," referring not just to those who are normally shown on state television but also to men in jeans and T-shirts, with gelled and styled hair and women in looser hijabs, with makeup, and tight and colorful clothes.

This distinction is so important that in 2014 for the annual Jerusalem Day march to show support for Palestinians, the gheyr-e khodis staged a march the day *before* the official government-sponsored march to show their opposition to Israel's ongoing attacks against Gaza that summer. They wanted to protest Israel's latest aggressions, but they did not want to be associated with pro-regime supporters and the regime's rhetoric on Israel. Many of Iran's independent filmmakers, such as Jafar Panahi, participated in the unofficial gheyr-e khodi march, as did prominent women's rights activists, writers, and artists.

The 2009 protests had laid bare these fault lines. Amir-Youssefi, in an attempt to deflect the conversation away from who best represented "the people," said, "This film is not even about 2009; this is about the frictions in the 1980s."

The *Kayhan* journalist responded, "Then you need to show that Monir's leftist brother wasn't executed in prison." He turned his body directly toward Amir-Youssefi, "You cannot refer to those executions."

For many regime supporters, the execution of thousands of political activists in the 1980s—the so-called counterrevolutionaries—remains a contentious issue that they do not know how to address.[5] How to manage and contain the fact that other groups fought alongside the Islamists to rid the country of the Shah but were later thrown into prison and executed for being "counterrevolutionaries" is a dilemma that continues to stump regime supporters. Admitting their existence goes against the grain of the Islamic Republic's history that the 1979 Revolution was an "Islamic Revolution" and that there was nearly universal support for Khomeini. Rewriting the history of the revolution or depicting the "counterrevolutionaries" as puppets of the West or the Soviet Union or as traitors (as in the case of the Mujaheddin-e Khalq organization) have been the main tropes in the regime's media. Thus, any mention of them and their stories should simply be erased, as the men in the room suggested.

"I have a recommendation on how to fix that part of the film and not refer to the political executions in the prison," Mostafa said. "Have the brother kill himself in prison. That way, you're not depicting any political executions, but showing how weak these counterrevolutionaries were by committing suicide." The other journalists readily agreed with the suggestion. For the first time that night, the mood in the room improved as they felt that they had come up with a solution to mend the film. Although journalists and Basiji student leaders, they took on the role of the censor.

"That works [having the brother commit suicide], because one of the best scenes of the film was where the counterrevolutionary brother tells his Basiji nephew to take care of his mom, because 'you all stayed on the scene, while we've been eliminated from the scene,'" the *Kayhan* journalist said. That scene in the film accused the regime of murdering and exiling the opposition, but instead, this journalist chose to read it as if the counterrevolutionary had admitted to no longer caring for his country and, therefore, preferred to abandon it.

The gathering had gone into its fifth hour. It was nearing 10:00 p.m., and Mr. Hosseini drew the meeting to a close, reiterating how important it was to have these "two sides" sit and talk with each other in a private setting, with the goal of coming to a mutual understanding. As we got up to go, Mr. Hosseini took each reporter aside and tried to convince him further not to publish anything negative about the film. "That only hurts our cause and makes this film more popular," he told each of them. The journalists finally agreed and left the room with smiles on their faces.

Leaving Sureh that night, Amir-Youssefi offered Mr. Hosseini and me a ride. The streets were no longer clogged with traffic. As Amir-Youssefi cruised at a comfortable speed through central Tehran, Mr. Hosseini talked excitedly. "This was a really incredible meeting, Mohsen."

"No, it wasn't! These kids are way too closed-minded and ideological. They were crazy with their suggestions!" Amir-Youssefi responded.

"I know," Mr. Hosseini replied, "but this was good. You'll see. This will be good for you and your film. Just change the scene where the Greens are in Monir's yard. Make it shorter and put music over the sounds of the motorcycles. Make sure to make any beatings of the protestors inaudible."

"So, basically, you want me to change history," Amir-Youssefi responded.

The Revolutionary Divide

The insider/outsider divide is common in postrevolutionary regimes, and much has been written about it in other revolutionary contexts, though less in Iran. In Iran, this divide exists for not only international enemies (*doshman*, i.e., the United States) but also domestic ones (gheyr-e khodi), who at times can be reformed into "good citizens" but at other times cannot. Similar to this divide in other postrevolutionary contexts, the khodi/gheyr-e khodi classification in Iran, as articulated by the regime, distinguishes "outsider" (gheyr-e khodi) both as a term within the political imaginary and as a threat *to* the political imaginary. In other words, the political imaginary of the Islamic Republic needs the figure of the gheyr-e khodi. If the gheyr-e khodi were to disappear altogether, it would threaten to dissolve the revolutionary collective itself. Precisely for this reason, regime cultural institutions spend significant time and resources in propagating this divide.[6] Yet, the gheyr-e khodi is useful not only in the political imaginary; the demarcation also has profound social and structural repercussions in postrevolutionary Iran.

Distinctions between those who are khodi (us, or literally "self") and those who are gheyr-e khodi (them, or literally "not-self, not-us") go back to demarcations of family ties and religious and ethnic groups in modern Iran.[7] Khodis are those who are connected via kinship networks, and they play a large role in marriage, land ownership, and allegiances. Throughout the twentieth century, as Iranian society became more and more urbanized and as relationships began to be defined based on professional affiliations, the scope of khodi expanded to include people in one's professional social circle.[8]

Like any social category, being a khodi or a gheyr-e khodi is marked by processes of exclusion, and, as frequently happens for many cultural frames, it is a fluid association that changes based on time, place, and circumstance. One can be a khodi to a group in one circumstance but then treated as a gheyr-e khodi in another. This is often the case in the cultural realm in the Islamic Republic, where an artist can be supported at one time but later shunned because of a particular work of art or statement.[9]

The boundaries of khodi can also change rapidly. After the reformists won elections in the late 1990s in Iran, more hard-line factions in the Islamic Republic began to claim that the reformists were no longer khodis. With members of Ayatollah Khomeini's family on their side, the reformists have challenged hard-liners about this claim. It continues to be a contentious debate within the various factions of the Islamic Republic, and it plays itself out in the cultural realm among regime artists, as well as between different generations of regime supporters. The stakes are high, because who is included in the revolutionary collective defines what the regime is.

Structurally Embedding the Khodi/Gheyr-e Khodi Divide

After the establishment of the Islamic Republic, as various political and social groups vied for power, the new government used the khodi/gheyr-e khodi distinction as a way to protect its newfound power and to weed out its opposition. In the early days of the revolution, the khodi/gheyr-e khodi distinction was visually demarcated. With new rules on men's and women's attire, the gheyr-e khodis were easier to spot; outward appearance was a significant sign of belonging. For men, being a khodi—and therefore an ideal revolutionary Islamic citizen—meant having the right amount of facial hair and correct dress. Men should have stubble on their faces or, better yet, a beard. Clean-shaven men were called seh-tiqe (literally, someone who shaves with a three-blade razor).[10] Additionally, the style of dress for men became increasingly important. In an attempt to do away with "frivolous" Western fashions, which had been advocated in the Shah's regime, the Islamic Republic outlawed neckties. Under the Shah, state-run television and print media officially promoted Western dress while degrading Iranian and Islamic dress as "backwards." The emphasis on promoting certain Iranian and Islamic dress after the revolution came in large part as a reaction to the Shah's sartorial policies.[11] In the first decade of the revolution, wearing a necktie could result in a costly fine. Men who wore ties were condescendingly referred to as *kerevāti* (tie wearers) by supporters of the Islamic Republic. Instead, the new government promoted collarless dress shirts, or *yakneh ākhundi* (cleric's collar), resembling the collarless style of shirts clerics wear in Iran.

In the first two decades of the revolution and in some circles to this day, a hezbollahi style of dress is a fully buttoned, collarless, long-sleeve shirt that is not tucked into the man's slacks, and black dress shoes, sometimes with the back of the shoe folded inwards to create a slipper look, denoting piety.[12] Denim jeans were deemed "too Western" in the first decade of the revolution, although today, some regime supporters wear denim. For women, dress is a constant game of cat-and-mouse with the authorities.[13] In the first decade after the revolution, the ideal revolutionary Islamic female citizen wore a black chador or a black *maghna'e* under which not a single strand of hair could be seen.[14] Today, it is much more acceptable for female regime supporters to wear colorful headscarves and light overcoats, though they must still be fully covered. Khodi women also refrain from wearing nail polish, and if they wear slacks, they also wear stockings so as to minimize the amount of bare skin.[15]

It is significant that these regulations were often codified. In other words, the visual demarcations of khodi/gheyr-e khodi were structurally embedded in the policing apparatus of the state. There were serious threats of fines, lashings, and even prison time for failing to dress appropriately, especially in the first two decades after the revolution. In addition, certain employment opportunities, especially in state organizations, have been predicated on at least looking and acting "as if" one was a khodi. Potential employees for regime cultural centers and state universities are subjected to extensive screening (discussed in chapter 2), including interviews with neighbors and family members. Thus, the khodi/gheyr-e khodi divide has legal, material, and social consequences in postrevolutionary Iran. It has played a critical role in restructuring political and social power in Iran.

"Othering" Intellectuals

The *rowshanfekrs* to which Mr. Hosseini and the journalists referred dismissively throughout the meeting are not simply intellectuals in the Euro-American sense of the term. In Iran the term signals the educated, salaried middle class, which sees itself as different from the traditional population, as well as from the merchant, *bazāri* middle class.[16] The idea of the intellectual has a long history in contemporary Iran, and in the Islamic Republic this notion has been further complicated by an exponential rise in the proportion of the population that is university educated.[17] Nonetheless, it is telling that regime cultural producers, who are often well educated, do not consider themselves—nor are they considered—rowshanfekrs.[18] Popularly, the term connotes more than just education and cosmopolitanism; it also includes notions of cultural and social capital, including comportment, social circle, and dress.[19]

Elite artists with connections abroad, or those championed by the secular Iranian diaspora, fare well in international circles. Having one's film travel to international film festivals is an important marker for filmmakers the world over. Regime filmmakers face a particular obstacle in participating in film festivals because sanctions make it impossible for them to have credit cards, which are necessary for submitting festival fees. Throughout my research, I met only a handful of regime cultural producers who had family abroad that could lend a credit card for festival fees. Gheyr-e khodi filmmakers, on the other hand, tend to have at their disposal a vast network of family and friends abroad for such tasks. From the point of view of regime filmmakers, the work of gheyr-e khodis circulates internationally, while their films do not.[20] They attribute this to the soft war (*jang-e narm*) waged against them by the West and especially by the Iranian diaspora media. As Mr. Hosseini said to the journalists at the meeting, "We all know that eventually this film will be screened, and even if it's banned, one of the Iranian satellite stations will beam it into Iran and everyone will watch it and it will become even more popular that way."

The Dilemma of the Regime Cultural Producers

In the end, Amir-Youssefi did not change any of the scenes, refusing to censor his film any more than he already had. He told me that he did not care about what the guys in that room had to say about the details of his film, because they "don't know what they're talking about." Instead, he acknowledged that he just had to keep them happy for long enough so they would not shut down his film completely. Amir-Youssefi and other gheyr-e khodis recognize that in these instances, despite not having formal power, they wield social and cultural capital.

The day after that private meeting with the journalists, the Fajr Film Festival notified Amir-Youssefi that his film would be shown. Mr. Hosseini took that as a sign of success. In the days leading up to the festival, however, the festival organizers changed their minds again. They would screen the film, they said, but they would not let the film be considered in the competition. Amir-Youssefi refused and proposed a compromise: the film wouldn't be shown at Fajr but would be officially cleared to be screened in cinemas after the Iranian new year in March. Fajr ostensibly agreed, although instead of being allowed to show at cinemas, the film was banned altogether.[21] In response, Amir-Youssefi then began doing interviews with both the Iranian and the Iranian diaspora press, explaining how his work had been censored and how he had been treated by regime figures. Although Amir-Youssefi's cultural capital as a filmmaker rose—he became known as the brave filmmaker who pushed back against regime censorship—his film did not garner an audience.

In subsequent meetings where I saw Mostafa, whenever the topic of Amir-Youssefi and his film came up, he became visibly irritated and his voice rose. He complained that the diaspora press had once again depicted the regime cultural producers unfairly. Their worldview, he said, was constantly under attack by gheyr-e khodis and intellectuals. "Mr. Hosseini wanted us to be kind and fair to Amir-Youssefi, and we were. But in return, he only bad-mouthed us to the press, and all the satellite stations call us dictatorial. That film's story was distorted and should not be screened! But for intellectual Iranians, we're the backward village idiots. They don't care that this film insults our sensibilities."

"I'll never participate in something like that again," Mostafa continued. "No matter how much Mr. Hosseini tries for dialogue, those intellectuals make us out to be the bad guys. That's how they treated us at the university too. I don't know why we should offer them an olive branch when they think we're just closed-minded idiots. They have no desire to engage with us. Why should we?"

Having spent time with Mostafa at the university before he graduated, I had seen how he and his friends were shunned by the other students. Especially in an art university in Iran, where style of dress and comportment are important indicators of one's outlook, Mostafa and his friends were made to feel that they did not fit in. The art (*honari*) style of dress, which in the fifteen years of the new millennium had first been a bohemian style and later a hipster style for both men and women, became the predominant look for aspiring young artists and signaled a subculture at odds with the regime.[22] This art style came to represent and define "cool" in urban Iran.[23]

From at least high school, Mostafa and his colleagues in the university Basij organization told me that not only had they *felt* excluded from that culture, but they actually *had been* excluded as the ultimate other. "They take one look at us and they automatically dismiss us and our work because of how we're dressed," Mansour, a nineteen-year old Basiji student in Mostafa's university told me. The angry looks the art students shot at Mostafa and his friends were not unwarranted; Mostafa and his organization spent a lot of energy policing their fellow classmates. Ironically, the very regulations that had been set up at the beginning of the Islamic Republic to create a revolutionary collective sharing certain ideals of dress and comportment now made supporters of the regime feel excluded in society at large.

Precisely for these reasons, the children of the first and second generation of the Basij and Revolutionary Guard try not to dress as if they come from pro-regime families (see chapter 1). Most of my interlocutors' daughters wore colorful headscarves and overcoats instead of chadors. The boys styled their hair and followed the latest trends at school. If their fathers were wounded veterans of the war, they faced scorn in secondary school and at the university level from other students, since offspring of wounded veterans get advantages in placement in the extremely competitive national university entrance exam.

For this reason, they attempted to hide any affiliation with the regime in their outward appearance. Boys whose fathers had made a fortune through the Revolutionary Guard's myriad business ventures went a step further, flaunting their luxurious lifestyle on Instagram, including alluding to their escapades with the opposite sex.

Regime cultural producers face a conundrum that results from the structural conditions of wielding power in a revolutionary government: they use their political power unapologetically, yet they lack social and cultural capital. This capital, especially in the art world, is often held by gheyr-e khodis who have easier access to international markets and the Iranian diaspora. Internally, gheyr-e khodi artists and intellectuals hold pride of place, and because they have been heavily censored and policed inside Iran, they end up retaliating socially against the regime supporters whom they blame for the censorship.

In this dynamic, regime cultural producers ultimately fall short in attempting to expand the revolutionary collective they fear is shrinking. They fall short for two reasons: First, they cannot agree on who should be included in the revolutionary collective and how flexible that inclusion should be. Second, because of the structural reinforcement of exclusion in postrevolutionary Iran, those who have been excluded often face grave material, social, and cultural consequences. This makes any attempt to bring people back into the revolutionary collective by those who are pro-regime an uphill battle.

4

New Strategies

FOUR YEARS HAD PASSED SINCE THE 2009 PROTESTS, and the Syrian civil war was raging. I had never had a chance to talk with Mr. Hosseini about *Elegy*, the film Mr. Ahmadi had given me about veterans in mental health institutions. I was eager to know his thoughts. When I asked him, he averted his gaze and looked to the ground before he said, "I know things are not great, and we need to improve. But how many homeless veterans exist in America?"

His initial reactions to many of my questions were to deflect them by pointing out similar problems in the United States. But days after my questions, he found a reason to invite me to his office to answer them. This time, Mr. Ahmadi was in his office as well. After drinking tea and exchanging pleasantries, Mr. Hosseini told me that he wanted to give me a new book that would be good for my research, but it was at a different office across town. "I'll take you; let's go in my car." The three of us walked to Mr. Hosseini's car.

I knew he didn't actually need to give me a book. A car ride was Mr. Hosseini's way of telling me things he didn't want his coworkers to hear. Cars are liminal private spaces in Iran where personal, political, and private matters can be discussed and explored.[1] In a society where outdoor spaces can be policed and where who is allowed in the private realm of homes comes layered with meaning—especially between the sexes—the car is the perfect "proper" space: private, yet public. In cars, the words of Mr. Hosseini and my other interlocutors were uncensored. There was no threat of anyone listening, and

Tehran's infamous traffic gave us the opportunity to spend long periods of time together in a sanctioned space.

Mr. Hosseini began, "I know we have a lot of problems with how our system has treated veterans. But what's our alternative? I want to push the regime to make things better. We need gradual reforms. Look, there are just too many outside forces that want to do us harm. You know the Mujaheddin was behind the 2009 Green Movement."

"The Mujaheddin?" I asked in surprise.

Mr. Hosseini was referring to the Mujaheddin-e Khalq Organization (MEK), the largest Iranian armed opposition movement, which advocates the overthrow of the Islamic Republic. The organization was founded in Iran in 1965 by a group of left-leaning Muslim university students. Its adherents played a role in toppling the Shah. But after Ayatollah Khomeini took power, they eventually turned their activities against the Islamic Republic. In the early 1980s, the MEK assassinated more than three hundred high-ranking officials in the Islamic Republic. These included the regime's popularly elected president Mohammad Ali Rajai, the prime minister, the head of the judiciary, dozens of members of parliament, and high-ranking clerics. The current Supreme Leader, Ali Khamenei, barely escaped an assassination attempt by the MEK in 1981. While he was giving a sermon, a bomb planted in a tape recorder exploded, severely injuring his arm, vocal cords, and lungs. He was left without the ability to use his right hand. For many in the Islamic Republic's leadership, opposition to the MEK is personal. As a result, the Mujahedin suffered heavy losses in the first decade of the revolution, when many members were imprisoned and executed.

After the revolution, the organization became increasingly cultish under the leadership of Masoud Rajavi and later his wife, Maryam Rajavi. From 1986 until 2012, the MEK ran an army base in Iraq called Camp Ashraf, from which it helped coordinate attacks against Iran with the Iraqi army. Although the United States, the European Union, Canada, and the United Kingdom designated the MEK as a terrorist organization in the late 1990s and early 2000s, it was taken off these lists between 2009 and 2012. Around the same time, the organization began to spend heavily on lobbying in the West, especially in the United States, and has paid tens of thousands of dollars

to high-level American politicians in both political parties. Due to its lobbying efforts and its material support from states such as Saudi Arabia, the
MEK continues to be a national security threat for the Islamic Republic, even
though the organization is much smaller now than it was at the beginning
of the revolution.

The MEK has been a straw man for the Islamic Republic from its inception, but new depictions of the MEK as fierce and untrustworthy gained
considerable traction with the rise of the Green Movement. Iran's Ministry
of Intelligence put pressure on regime cultural producers—claiming that the
MEK, with its Saudi, Israeli, and American backers, was responsible for the
unrest of the Green Movement—and asked state television to create a public
awareness campaign about the organization. The Ministry of Intelligence
offered funding for media that dealt with this theme. The goal, as Mr. Hosseini articulated to me, was to "prevent our population from going down this
slippery slope again."

"You can't understand what this organization is capable of," Mr. Hosseini
said to me.

Sitting in the back seat, I leaned forward and looked toward Mr. Ahmadi:
"Even after what happened to you at the protests, you believe this?"

Mr. Ahmadi turned to look me in the eye and said with concern, "Look how
easily foreign groups duped Syrians and hijacked that movement. If the Islamic
Republic hadn't acted the way it did in 2009, I guarantee you the Mujahedin
and outside forces would be wreaking havoc in Iran right now."

"But the Mujaheddin didn't make *you* go into the streets!" I said in disbelief to Mr. Ahmadi.

"No, they didn't, but they laid the groundwork of misinformation that
led me to believe in the movement," he replied. "Look, I believe in [reformist
candidate Mir Hussein] Mousavi and I'm glad I voted for him, and I don't
think he needs to be under house arrest right now. But the unrest after the
vote was fomented by the MEK."

It later came to light that just as the Green Movement was erupting in
Iran, the infamous Stuxnet cyberattacks targeting Iran's uranium enrichment facilities had also been launched.[2] In the first instance of a widespread
cyberwar launched by Israel and the United States, Stuxnet wreaked havoc

and confusion in the military and intelligence community inside Iran. The malware caused centrifuges in Iran's uranium enrichment plants to blow up, with no indication in the computer systems that they were malfunctioning. Thus, Iranian engineers had no idea the centrifuges were not spinning at the right speed until it was too late. Stuxnet, a computer virus, was not uncovered until 2010 and was kept from the public until 2012. From the point of view of the Iranian regime, it was extremely suspect that in the same days in 2009 that the streets exploded in the largest protests since the 1979 Revolution, their prized nuclear facilities were also under attack. For the intelligence community inside the country, the two events became linked. And given that the MEK had provided intelligence about Iran's nuclear program to Israel and the United States in the past, many within the regime concluded that the MEK had caused the chaos both on the streets and in the nuclear facilities.

"Look," Mr. Hosseini said, locking eyes with me in the rearview mirror, "you know my wife and children voted for Mousavi and protested in the Green Movement, too. But we've now realized that the Mujahedin played a large role in encouraging the unrest in the country. We have to stand strong, or we'll turn into Syria."

Although there is little evidence that young people in Iran are persuaded by the armed opposition organization, the MEK has become a scapegoat for all forms of opposition to the Islamic Republic. Moreover, because the MEK continued to receive funds and support from the United States and Saudi Arabia, including for media campaigns against Iran, and it continued to give intelligence about Iran to Israel, Saudi Arabia, and Western powers, the Islamic Republic continued its media campaign against the organization.

Mr. Ahmadi continued, "Why should our youth be duped into following opposition groups? Sure, we have problems that need fixing, and you know how deeply I believe that, Ms. Bajoghli. But our young people need to understand that these things can be fixed internally."

"We have to ensure that organizations like the Mujaheddin aren't able to influence our internal affairs," Mr. Hosseini interjected. "I don't mean to be rude, but don't be naïve. Syria isn't a civil war. It's being funded by many sides. And the MEK wants the same thing in Iran. The Mujaheddin and its American and Saudi backers are much more pernicious than you think."

"You won't believe what our younger filmmakers have found on them," Mr. Ahmadi said. "Come to the studios next week and I'll show you the latest films we've been making on this organization."

New Productions

I took Mr. Ahmadi up on his invitation. The production office of one of the studios working on anti-MEK films was located off Keshavarz Boulevard, in an alleyway that led toward Palestine Square. It occupied one floor of a typical 1950s Tehrani villa, with high ceilings, sturdy stone steps, and large windows. About seven filmmakers had offices on the second floor, though they were never there at the same time. It was a hub for young regime filmmakers. With financial backing from producers such as Mr. Ahmadi, these young filmmakers fared well in the larger media world of documentary filmmaking in Iran. Although documentary filmmaking requires a substantially smaller budget than narrative filmmaking, producers such as Mr. Ahmadi were crucial because all seven of the filmmakers in this studio (as in all the regime studios where I spent time) were full-time documentary filmmakers. The funding and distribution plans that Mr. Ahmadi could secure due to his connections were necessary for these young men who financially supported their families.

One October morning in 2013, four of us squeezed into the office of Morteza Payeshenas to discuss his new film, *An Unfinished Film for My Daughter Somayeh* (*Film-e Nātamāmi Barā-ye Dokhtaram Somayeh*). Two of the men were directors/editors in the same production office, and one, Mr. Saeedi, was in charge of programming the "Sacred Defense" films for the upcoming Cinema Verité Film Festival, Iran's preeminent documentary film festival. Mr. Hosseini had encouraged Mr. Saeedi to watch *An Unfinished Film for My Daughter Somayeh* (figure 1) and to schedule it for the festival. Payeshenas, thirty years of age, hesitated to screen the unfinished film at the festival, but Mr. Ahmadi and Mr. Hosseini had insisted that he do so, as it would mean more financial support and visibility for the production studio.

Mostafa Mohammadi, the protagonist of the documentary, had filmed nearly every aspect of his family's life with his camcorder. Payeshenas uses this home footage as the main material of the film, and in doing so, he not

FIGURE 1. Film poster for *An Unfinished Story for My Daughter Somayeh*. Director: Morteza Payehshenas, 2015

only tells the story from the father's point of view but also positions the film as an intimate first-person narrative. *Somayeh* is about the Mohammadi family, supporters of the MEK whose two older children are interned at Camp Ashraf, a military compound in Iraq. The film follows the father as he struggles to get his children, Somayeh and Mohammad, back home to Canada. Camp Ashraf is a small city that also served as a military base and headquarters for the MEK. Built in 1986 in Iraq's Diyala Province, about fifty miles west of the Iranian border, the camp was meant to be a base from which the MEK would support Saddam Hussein's forces against Iran during the Iran-Iraq War.

Mostafa, a refugee from the revolution, enrolled his daughter in the youth school of the MEK in Canada. That school decided to take some of the students to visit Camp Ashraf, and the family's footage shows them happily bidding Somayeh farewell at the airport on her way to Iraq. Somayeh does not return from that school trip and communicates to her family that she has chosen to stay at Camp Ashraf. The parents claims that they were tricked by the MEK into sending their daughter and that she has been brainwashed to stay. They have little communication from her for a year and are not allowed to visit. The following year, Somayeh's younger brother, Mohammad, decides to volunteer for Camp Ashraf to check on his sister and vows to come back with her in tow. He leaves for Iraq and is not allowed to leave the camp either.

Despite multiple trips to France and Jordan to meet with MEK officials, the family is denied the right to visit them. It is only in 2003, when Mostafa Mohammadi attempts to immolate himself to protest MEK leader Maryam Rajavi's arrest in Europe, that the organization deems him loyal enough. They give him, his wife, and their younger child the right to visit the camp. According to the documentary, the Mohammadi family is one of the few families ever allowed inside Camp Ashraf. The father records the entire trip on his camcorder.

During this visit, Mostafa learns that his son, Mohammad, was raped at the camp. The father petitions the Canadian government to intervene on behalf of his son, a Canadian citizen. In the same scene in which his son writes an appeal to the Canadian government, Mostafa also records Somayeh writing a letter to the Canadian government asking for its assistance in her return. The family knows this may be in vain, as Somayeh had not yet obtained her Canadian citizenship before she left for Iraq. Their son eventually returns to Canada with his family, but Somayeh is denied leave by the MEK.

According to the film, upon Mohammad's release, the MEK increases pressure on Somayeh to distance herself from the family. When Mostafa returns to Camp Ashraf to visit his daughter, Somayeh refuses to see him and tells her family to leave her alone. In a last-ditch effort, her father meets with American military personnel in Iraq to enlist their help. They tell him that since Somayeh is over eighteen years of age, they cannot help him. The film ends with the family watching old home videos of when Somayeh was still with them and wondering if she will ever return home.

Interwoven with the family's story are interviews with former MEK members who were at Camp Ashraf but managed to escape or be released. Their interviews touch upon the gender politics of the organization, especially sexual harassment. According to one interviewer, Beeta Rasouli, women were forced to undress in front of the group's leader, Masoud Rajavi. Other members talk about being duped by the MEK to go to Camp Ashraf and not being allowed to leave or communicate with their families in Iran or in the West once they arrived. The film shows footage that Payeshenas filmed outside Camp Ashraf: fathers and mothers stand at the gates of the camp, screaming their children's names over megaphones and pleading for them to come out.

The MEK claims that the Islamic Republic has paid for these families to come from Iran to protest and that many of the children the families are looking for are actually not in Ashraf but were executed by the Islamic Republic in the prisons in the 1980s for being a part of the MEK. When I asked the filmmaker about these allegations, he denied them. He said the family members come on their own. When I asked why the women in the footage wear the distinctive hijab of officialdom in the Islamic Republic (*maghna'e*) rather than headscarves or even chadors, he said he did not know and moved on to discussing other parts of the film.[3]

As I watched the film, I got a feeling that anything except for the Islamic Republic is scary and is there to trick and dupe people. I shared this feeling with Payeshenas and he smiled, acknowledging that this was the goal of his film. It is an attempt to discourage frustrated youth from joining just "any opposition movement."

In my time in the studio with the filmmaker, the main element he used to make the film feel like an independent film was a voice-over narration from the father's point of view. Payeshenas wrote the narration and voiced it himself. He worked for hours every day preparing the narration and spent nearly a year recording, editing, and rerecording the voice-over. Because he did not edit out any of the scenes where the father uses profane language to describe the Islamic Republic, the documentary feels like an anti-regime film. Given these editorial choices, viewers could not easily detect that it was a regime production.[4]

The Regime Goes Underground

In the meeting in his studio, Payeshenas sat at the keyboard in the editing suite with his back to us. On one of his two large monitors were frames of the film, and on the other, he made notes with his Adobe Premiere editing software as we gave feedback. We had already watched the film and had begun discussing it scene by scene.

"Why does your narration refer to them as 'the Organization' [sāzmān] rather than 'the hypocrites' [monāfeqin]?" Mr. Saeedi asked as soon as the film ended, referring to the term the regime preferred when talking about the MEK.

Payeshenas, expecting this question, responded with assurance, "I really don't want people to see this and think it's propaganda. Then they'll just stop watching it. If I used 'the hypocrites' in the narration, the viewer would instantly know this is a regime film. I want the viewer to think that the narration is from the father's point of view. I don't want the viewer to know we made the film." Payeshenas readily admitted his attempt at dissimulation. Without it, he contended, the audience would not engage with the material. For general audiences in Iran, a film produced by the regime or its cultural centers is almost always seen as propaganda. The new strategy is to remove as many fingerprints of regime cultural centers as possible.

Payeshenas's producers consciously chose the route of dissimulation in their distribution strategies in order to ensure that the film would travel as an "underground" film. Underground films enjoy a certain prestige because of their transgressive nature. After witnessing multiple debates about the film's distribution, I noticed that it began to circulate on burned VCDs in floppy plastic envelopes. It was being sold by Iranian street vendors who usually carry contraband films. Five artists who define themselves as anti-regime each gave me the film in Iran and encouraged me to watch this "underground film" they had bought on the street. They said it was an incredible testament by former Mujaheddin members about the terrors of the organization.

In a class on screenwriting Mr. Hosseini taught at the Art University, he decided to show the film to see how students would react. Testing the film like this in university classrooms in Tehran was one of the ways Mr. Hosseini and his colleagues gauged whether their strategy of dissimulation was working. Mr. Hosseini introduced the film to the class as "an independent film that I just saw the other night. I had to show it to you all. I was left amazed with what I saw." He asked the students to write a letter from the point of view of Somayeh to her father.

"You let me down. Instead of protecting me as a father should, you let me go into the hands of those wolves. How could you leave me like that? It's not that I don't want to come back with you. It's that I can't. And the worst thing is you can't do anything about it. You can't save me. What kind of father are you?" Armineh read, her voice full of emotion.

Mr. Hosseini had screened other regime productions in the class, and the students usually dozed off in boredom, made up excuses for not completing the assignments, and rolled their eyes during discussions. This was the first time all semester that I saw them come to class enthusiastically and share their writing. *Somayeh* seemed to have deeply affected them. No one was able to tell that it had been created by a regime film crew.

The three young women in the class, in particular, wrote scathing letters to Somayeh's father. Armineh's voice broke as she read her letter, calling the father a coward. After class, Mr. Hosseini said to me, "Armineh's letter was amazing, wasn't it? You can feel the power of this film in people like her. She's Armenian. If this film can affect a non-Muslim Iranian in that way, then we're doing something right," Mr. Hosseini said proudly as he packed his briefcase.

All six students spoke about the horrors of the MEK. "I can't believe people join its ranks," Danyal, one of the students, said to the class during discussion. The others nodded in agreement. "This is not how Iranians should act," Daryoush chimed in.

Despite Payeshenas's attempts at dissimulation, however, key scenes and interviews could throw *Somayeh*'s authenticity as an "independent" film into question. For example, in one of the interviews done in Europe with MEK members, the daughter of a former MEK member wears a loosely draped hijab. It was obvious to me that she does not wear a hijab on a regular basis but was asked to do so because she was being filmed by a regime film crew. When I asked Payeshenas, he admitted that when they arrived at the house, the daughter, Nooshin, was wearing a T-shirt that showed tattooed arms, and her hair was not covered. Knowing that this film could air on state television one day, he asked her to cover her arms and wear a hijab.

Another possible giveaway is the fact that some of the former MEK members interviewed for the film have also appeared in state television pieces against the MEK. This would be apparent only to viewers who have also seen the television documentaries about the MEK; in general, the interviews come across as singular and convincing. One interviewee in particular, Mohammad Hussein Sobhani, appears in other anti-MEK films that Payeshenas directed, as well in as many films broadcast on state television about the MEK.[5] Sobhani has been accused by opposition groups, not just the MEK, of collaborating with the Islamic Republic. Although I recognized him immediately, given that I was watching regime films constantly for research, I never heard this criticism raised by viewers, either at the Art University or a variety of public screenings of the film that I attended. Payeshenas denied that any of the people filmed were collaborators with the regime, and he insisted that the stories told by the former MEK members who now live in Iran were narrated without any kind of pressure.

Creating Bigger Audiences

Buoyed by the positive experience of screening *Somayeh* at the Art University, Mr. Hosseini screened *The Best Statue in the World* (*Behtarin mojasameh-ye donyā*, 2011) the following week. Directed by Habib Ahmadzadeh, *The Best Statue in the World* is a comedic biopic about Darya-Gholi, who by all accounts was a drunk, a gambler, and a thug before the war. Despite Darya-Gholi's disobedient ways, he is credited with saving Abadan from the Iraqis, as he was the first person to see the invading army marching toward Abadan from Khorramshahr. He rode his bike to the Revolutionary Guard commander in Abadan and informed him of the incursion. The film argues that Darya-Gholi essentially saved Abadan from falling into the hands of the Iraqis. He was killed shortly afterward in battle.

A statue in an Abadan square commemorates Darya-Gholi, but as the film shows, no one remembers who he was or what the statue stands for. Throughout the film, Darya-Gholi's spirit provides comedic narration as he "sees" his city and watches his friends after his death, dismayed that no one remembers his act. The film is meant to be a commentary on the fact that the state's official narrative of the war has actually created a desire to forget the war rather than to remember it and its heroes, Ahmadzadeh explained to me. And his main goal, he stated, was to show that "no one is perfect all the time. Instead, with Darya-Gholi, I wanted to show a deeply flawed man, someone who was a real thug but had the guts and bravery to act like Imam Hossein at the most crucial moment. That's what our youth need to learn. Can they act like heroes when it's most needed?" Despite these lofty goals, the film did not do well with audiences. *The Best Statue in the World* takes a moralistic tone that is reminiscent of other official war films.

Mr. Hosseini thought the comedic narration would resonate with the students. Instead, they dozed off and passed notes to one another. When Mr. Hosseini left the room in the middle of the screening to take a phone call, the students began complaining: "Why are we watching this?" "We've been seeing these films on television all our lives." "What's the point of this screening?"

After the film, Mr. Hosseini asked the students what they thought, and they all politely answered that they liked it. "So, do you all want to go to Abadan and see the statue?"

"No," a female student at the front of the room said to him. "We already saw it in the film. That's enough for us." At that point, the hallway outside the screening room had begun to buzz with excited chatter as other students moved to their next classes. The students in the screening room got up, leaving Mr. Hosseini in midsentence.

Months later, Mr. Hosseini and Mr. Ahmadi coordinated a private meeting in parliament to meet with members of the Culture Committee. Mr. Hosseini told the members, many of whom he knew personally, "You all have failed for twenty-six years to tell our story to our younger generation. Let us try now. Give us one year. If we mess up, it's just one year to all the twenty-six years you all have messed up."

"I shocked them," he told me, laughing in his office later that day. "But we got them to give us 10 million US dollars to distribute these films to schools around the country." When I asked him what type of proposal he presented to the parliamentary committee to get that kind of money, he joked, "What do you mean by 'proposal'? I just talked to them and convinced them. They know me!" Mr. Hosseini's answer further illustrates the ad hoc nature of regime cultural planning in Iran and the importance of networks and connections in getting support for cultural work.

The funding was to be used for two purposes: first, to send regime films to all high school teachers in Tehran, and second, to create film festivals in smaller towns and provinces aimed at young audiences. Mr. Hosseini elaborated, "We'll send *The Best Statue in the World*, along with *Somayeh, Memories for All Seasons*,[6] and *The Wolves* to all high school teachers around the country. We'll encourage them to show these films in their classrooms. We'll also create more film festivals for small towns that don't have cinemas."

The Wolves (*Gorg-hā*) is a documentary that has played a large role in establishing "proof" of the MEK's complicity with foreign enemies of Iran. Originally a four-part series, it screened repeatedly on national television, but it did not have large audiences. Under advice from the likes of Mr. Hosseini, the editors recut *The Wolves* in 2013 from a multi-episode made-for-television documentary series down to a ninety-minute film. The producers issued this version on DVD and broadcast it on national television for two weeks. For two years, regime filmmakers lobbied the Education Ministry to include the shortened version of *The Wolves* in the high school curriculum, finally succeeding in 2014.

For regime filmmakers, the film plays a crucial role: it provides historical proof that the Islamic Republic is right in its distrust and hatred of not only the MEK but also any Iranian opposition group that can receive foreign funds to destabilize the regime. The film contains surveillance footage of MEK leaders meeting with intelligence teams from Saddam Hussein's government. The archival footage is from Iraqi intelligence films and archives, which Iran got access to after the fall of Saddam Hussein and the Baʿathist regime in 2003. The footage reveals the full extent of collaboration between the MEK and the Baʿathist regime.

Despite the funding that Mr. Hosseini received from parliament to distribute this film to high school teachers in Tehran, the teachers refused to show the film in their classrooms. Not only that, teachers began to refuse to show any of the films that they were sent. Despite the USD 10 million set aside for programs such as this, what Mr. Hosseini and his colleagues did not factor into their equation was that the teachers' union is one of the most organized in the country, and it constantly demands a more independent curriculum. The strategy of the regime filmmakers failed.

Ever the optimist, Mr. Hosseini quickly pivoted. He began to focus more of his energy on his second strategy, creating avenues for audiences outside Tehran and the major cities to watch regime films before they arrived in the major cities. He and Mr. Ahmadi focused on implementing two ideas: developing film festivals in provincial towns and changing how their films were broadcast on national television. In these ways, they hoped, they could reach nonurban viewers before the critics in Tehran had the chance to dismiss their films in national newspapers and magazines.

Mr. Hosseini and Mr. Ahmadi enlisted regime cultural centers to create ad hoc festivals on holidays in town centers with free soft drinks, sandwiches, and balloons, and an emcee to conduct entertainment before and after the screening. Posters for the festival are put up around town squares announcing the event. In the warmer months, a large screen and stage are set up outside. In the colder months, the events take place in an indoor space decorated with balloons and streamers and featuring loudspeakers that blast upbeat instrumental music.

Although the main goal of these events is to draw young people, the organizers face a number of obstacles. They aim to gain new young audiences, but they cannot offer what young people are looking for. I witnessed as they tried in vain to choose music geared to teenage and young adult audiences. Given the government's restrictions on pop music, the organizers are left with the choice of either playing instrumental music or children's songs.[7] If the organizers choose upbeat instrumental music, it often works "too well": young people begin to dance and become disappointed when the music stops and the film begins. At one event I attended, in order to avoid it turning into a dance party, the organizers began to play upbeat children's songs. The small children in the audience enjoyed this, but the teenagers and young adults sat back, unengaged and bored. Organizers sometimes invite a children's celebrity such as the children's television star Amoo Porang to serve as emcee and get the crowd going. And indeed, he would get the young children in the crowd and their parents clapping and singing. But once the films came on, the children became fidgety or fell asleep. The films that were being screened had been made for adult audiences and failed to engage the targeted audience of these ad hoc festivals. Yet, these festivals have been ongoing for five years now and the organizers believe that they are making an impact on the parents and teenagers. As for the younger children, Mr. Hosseini said, "They're now associating us with music and joy and celebration, not with death and mourning and martyrdom, like we did to the first two generations of the revolution."

The goal of these festivals is to provide a joyful atmosphere in towns where there is little opportunity for such gatherings and take advantage of the large number of assembled people to show "relevant" documentaries that the public "should" watch, such as films about the war against the opposition. Once the films travel in this fashion around smaller towns, they are then put on state television, but only on the provincial channels, not on Tehran's channel. The films are shown nightly for about a week or on a few consecutive Friday nights (depending on the film and the program schedule). Finally, these films are broadcast in Tehran, either at a film festival first (especially if the filmmakers do not want the audience to know they were made by pro-regime filmmakers), or directly on state television.[8]

By undertaking this counterintuitive strategy, in which audiences in Tehran are the last to see the films, the producers ensure that critical Iranian diaspora media do not start criticizing a film before it has a chance to circulate.[9] "By the time the stations abroad catch wind of the film, we've already shown it to most of the country," one producer told me with a smile. "They're too late to the game by that point."

Imagined Audiences

While it has become commonplace to venture that the construction of national identity as an imagined community relies upon widely circulated and shared media, from novels and films to newspapers and social media, the empirical audience is an unknown but taken-for-granted set of people.[10] It falls within the same category as "the population," "the nation," or "the masses."[11] As Raymond Williams argues, the notion of "the masses" is illusory in and of itself: there are no masses, "only ways of seeing people as masses."[12] Ien Ang argues, "In a similar vein, the 'television audience' only exists as an imaginary entity, an abstraction constructed from the vantage point of the institutions, in the interest of the institutions."[13]

Iran's regime filmmakers imagine their audiences, mainly the youth they wish to target, as abstractions. Regime filmmakers in Iran, much like Bollywood directors and filmmakers in other parts of the world, do not rely on audience measurement systems like the U.S. Nielsen ratings. Rather, they try to put themselves in the position of a potential young audience member who does not agree with the Islamic Republic.[14] Although some regime filmmakers and bigger cultural centers in Iran do commission audience research, I never saw the directors actually peruse those reports. Instead, the producers operate based on their assumptions about Iran's young people. They project onto their country's imagined youth their own wishes for the future of the Islamic Republic. And they imagine that Iranian young people will welcome this future if only they can be exposed to enough "correct" media.[15]

Barry Dornfeld notes in his study of American public television that producers act as surrogate audience members, "putting themselves in the place of their potential audience as they react to the material they are shaping into programs."[16] Regime filmmakers in Iran use the same approach. In effect, they rely on their own subjectivity to play the role of the surrogate audience member. As in Dornfeld's description of American public television producers, they end up "reacting to material they shoot and edit as viewers themselves, and often falling back on their subjective responses to defend these reactions."[17]

Crucially, given that most of the regime filmmakers are men, I witnessed repeatedly that they talk about their audiences as young men. These regime producers are most concerned with making sure young men can stand up and defend the nation against any aggression, and they define that defense through local understandings of masculinity.[18] The films they make feature male protagonists, while the women in the films are in supporting roles as mother or wife. The only times I heard them speak about young female viewers was when discussing who would play the male lead: they imagined that young women would come to watch the film if they cast a handsome lead actor. No other reference was made to female audiences.

Because they base filmmaking decisions on their beliefs about young male audiences, these regime production offices seek to attract as many young filmmakers as possible, believing that these young filmmakers can better understand their own generation and thus help make media targeted at them. Filmmakers such as Payeshenas are valuable in this cultural cosmos. He is critical of many of the same things that his peers who are not pro-regime object to, such as social restrictions, especially those targeted at women and youth. However, he believes these restrictions can eventually be reformed within the Islamic Republic. "There is a lot to criticize the Islamic Republic about," he explained. "I just don't want my generation to go into the arms of something worse just because they want change."

Though a supporter of the regime, Payeshenas is very critical of the crackdown on the Green Movement and even more critical of reformist politicians who are "not doing enough" in his view to push for change in Iran. His wife, a photographer by training, wears her hijab loosely, with her hair visible, indicating that she does not abide by the stricter interpretation of the regime for women's dress. Payeshenas talks regularly of his four-year-old daughter and cites her as his main reason for making these films about the MEK, in order to "wake up" the younger generations in Iran so that they won't fall for just any opposition movement against the regime. He regularly speaks about wanting a future for his daughter where she is able to advance in any field and not be held back by government restrictions against women. He chooses to make these films with the hopes of ensuring stability for the future of the country and for his daughter, above all else. For Payeshenas, this work is not about creating "propaganda." Instead, he sees it as necessary in a larger war of ideas in the Middle East over power and position.

5

Producing Nationalism

THE LEADERS OF THE REGIME'S MEDIA CENTERS had gathered for their monthly meeting. One prominent producer in the room said to his colleagues: "We have to learn to speak the language of youth and use their codes if we want them to like our work. We're speaking past them. How can we speak to them?"

As the regime's cultural producers were strategizing new engagement and distribution strategies, they began to brainstorm about the ways they could tailor the content of their work to young audiences. Their old stories were couched in their interpretations of a Shi'a ethos of fighting against oppression that was embodied in the Karbala mythology of Imam Hussein. But these stories clearly no longer resonated with their desired audience; they needed a new unifying story. This new story presented itself in the form of populist nationalism in the general population.

Mr. Ahmadi chimed in: "We have to show young people that we're here to protect Iran as a nation, not just the Islamic Republic as an idea. Young people pull away from us because they see the regime as alien to the history of Iran. We have to show them that *we* also care about Iran."

"Who is more Iranian than us? We're the only force in this country's history that's defended our nation's boundaries. We didn't give up even a strip of land in our war, unlike those corrupt monarchs!" a Revolutionary Guard commander in the room shot back.

"It's true," Mr. Hosseini responded, "but in our films and on our television series, all we've done is show our young people that we think about religion all day and cry for our martyrs. No one aspires to that—to be mourning all the time! No wonder they don't see that we're also nationalistic. Our story to them has always been a religious one. It's our own fault!"

"Look," Mr. Ahmadi interjected, "at how everyone seems to be naming their children after *Shāhnāmeh* characters . . ." The *Shāhnāmeh* (*Book of Kings*) is the long-form epic poem of the Persianate world written by Ferdowsi between 977 and 1010 CE. The *Shāhnāmeh* tells a mythical history of the pre-Islamic Persian Empire.

"It's true! I've read the *Shāhnāmeh* since I was fifteen, and I don't even know where they get some of these names from," Mr. Hosseini said, laughing. "They're trying so hard to identify with anything that is not Islamic that they're even willing to name their children these odd names," he chuckled.

"And the [Zoroastrian symbol] *farvahar* has become like the Christian cross! People wear it around their necks and put it on their key chains!" Mr. Ahmadi said.

"But Islam has been a part of Iran for 1,400 years! We're not going to erase that," the Revolutionary Guard commander said.

"No one said to erase it. Look, I know our people are still religious; they just don't want to show it the way that we tell them to anymore," Mr. Hosseini replied. "I don't blame them. Turn on state television today—it's one boring old cleric after another lecturing us on morality. And we all know they're lying between their teeth. They're all corrupt too and not a single one is without sin. No wonder we've become this boring thing young people don't identify with."

On the establishment of the Islamic Republic, an attempt was made to downplay Iranian holidays that were not Islamic. Citizens, however, did not oblige. Not only did they continue to celebrate the holidays rooted in Zoroastrianism, such as Nowruz (the Iranian new year, which is celebrated on the vernal equinox) and Yalda (the celebration of the winter solstice), but throughout the years, the celebrations have become more elaborate. Despite the implementation of a state-defined revolutionary identity that was framed through religion, there has been a movement driven by the population that emphasizes non-Islamic symbols of Iranian-ness. This is not to imply that people are rejecting religion; instead, they have moved towards defining "Iranian-ness" outside the official narrative of the state.[1]

Although none of the people in the room were supporters of then-president Mahmoud Ahmadinejad, Mr. Hosseini and Mr. Ahmadi suggested that they use Ahmadinejad's notion of "Iranian Islam" in their work, a notion that resituates the war and the regime in nationalist terms and attempts to take ownership of Islam away from the clerics. Nationalism has long played a role in the cultural productions of the Islamic Republic. Yet, after the Green Movement protests, regime cultural producers began to push for something more deliberate: they attempted to completely reimagine the Revolutionary Guard as an institution defending the Iranian nation, whereby nationalism— and not a political interpretation of Islam—was the Revolutionary Guard's driving force. It was a reframing of the Revolutionary Guard and the Basij as symbols. They were now meant to be national symbols, not just defenders of an Islamic revolution and regime. Regime media producers began to highlight this sentiment in their cultural productions from museums to films, books, and music.

A Museum for Populist Nationalism

As international pressures against Iran increased, including stifling sanctions imposed by the United States and Europe and an intensified proxy war with Saudi Arabia, this sense of populist nationalism continued to rise in Iran. Nowhere is this more evident than at the Sacred Defense Garden and Museum, a new megacomplex perched on the coveted hilltops of Abbasabad in Haqqani, north-central Tehran.

"The Islamic Republic is the only regime in the past two centuries in Iran that has not lost or signed away our national territory to foreign powers," museum guide Majid said as he pointed to a large map of Iran in an exhibition hall in the newly built, multimillion-dollar museum. "Look at all the land the corrupt Qajar dynasty sold for pennies and how the Shah gave away the Persian Gulf islands to the unworthy Arabs!" He pointed to a panel on the wall, showing the diminishing boundaries of Iran over the centuries. "When the Islamic Republic was in its infancy, we were attacked by a strong army backed by the West. We didn't know how to command the military yet and the other side had so many sophisticated weapons. But look at what we did for Iran—how we didn't lose even a strip of land to the Iraqis!"

The exhibition was filled with large maps that began with the expanse of the Persian Empire ruling swaths of Asia over three thousand years ago. It narrated Iran's ever-shrinking territory throughout the centuries: the country's contemporary size appears small in comparison to the glorified empire painted on the wall. The message of the museum was clear: leaders of previous Iranian kingdoms had recklessly given away territory throughout the centuries, thinking more about filling their own pockets than about the well-being of the nation. When the Islamic Republic was attacked by a strong enemy, it fought as a collective to maintain Iran's borders and, by extension, the nation's dignity as an ancient civilization. Majid stood back, wanting me to absorb the gravity of the presented narrative facts as I compared the maps on the wall.

This museum moved from celebrating martyrs—like the ubiquitous yet empty martyrs' museums that dot the map of Iran—to offering a narrative of nationalism, dignity, and pride. "We got Iran back from the hold of Western powers. We retook control of our country," Majid's coworker Fatemeh told me when we walked toward the third wing of the museum.

Majid, Fatemeh, and other young students and graduates were the museum's official guides. In an attempt to make the museum appealing to younger audiences, the museum's administration had purposefully hired and trained young guides to give the place a sense of youthful dynamism, one of the managers told me. Majid, a twenty-seven-year-old PhD student in history, was a member of the Basij, and his uncles had fought in the war. He was born immediately after the war ended, yet he talked about it as if he remembered every detail.

Fatemeh, a twenty-four-year-old guide who was also a member of her graduate school's Basij, told me: "When Iraq attacked with Western backing, we had nothing and we had to learn everything from scratch. But we did it, without any outside help or expertise."

"*We* built the bridges, *we* defended our nation, and *we* didn't lose any territory," Majid chimed in.

The Sacred Defense Garden and Museum, which opened in 2012, had been funded by the office of Mayor Baqer Qalibaf, a former commander of the Revolutionary Guard and a veteran of the war. The museum is part of a larger drive to modernize Tehran's architecture through new, futuristic structures, such as the award-winning Nature Bridge. Such projects point to broader aspirations to transform Tehran from a city dotted with gray buildings and endless murals of war martyrs to one boasting bright billboards and high-rises. The museum's park offers free access to anyone wanting to escape the capital's growing expanses of concrete. In the spring and summer, families from all political and social backgrounds picnic on the grounds.

To draw new audiences, the museum has invited independent artists to create exhibitions and installments, effectively courting the very people the Martyrs Museum pushed away for decades. Tanks and aircraft from the war are placed around the park, and in the back, a massive pool will later hold naval ships from the war with Iraq. The war is recast as a nationalist project in this museum rather than a religious quest, as it has been narrated in regime-produced martyrs' museums.

Mr. Ahmadi supported the premise and goals of the museum, even though he had personal disagreements with the men behind it: "We're all on the same page. For far too long, the regime has defined the war only for people that look like me. And now we all realize that we have to make the war attractive for all kinds of Iranians. Young people have to identify with it. If they don't identify with us, they'll eventually fight for something different to replace us."

Forefronting the Persian Gulf

In their effort to frame the revolution in terms of the nation, regime producers needed a national symbol that did not cross any of their religious red lines. They settled on the Persian Gulf. The struggle over the name of the Gulf—Persian or Arabian—has become a hotly politicized and nationalized fight between Iran, Saudi Arabia, and the Gulf nations. It is among the few issues that unite Iranians of different political stripes. Even in Los Angeles, a major hub of the Iranian diaspora and exiled community, large billboards began to appear throughout the city in 2012 after Google Maps labeled the body of water as simply "The Gulf." The billboards throughout Los Angeles claimed, "It is not The Gulf. It is the Persian Gulf." The pre-revolutionary flag appeared prominently on the billboards. The Islamic Republic has also invested heavily in this fight, not only launching public relations campaigns claiming the historical accuracy of the name Persian Gulf but also stating its claim over this body of water at international conferences and diplomatic meetings. The heavy presence of U.S. naval ships throughout the Gulf has made this body of water even more prominent in the national narrative of Iran.

I witnessed numerous debates between regime producers in which they lamented the fact that young Iranians spend so much time watching music videos from banned satellite stations. Music videos, they concluded, are how young people consume media today, and more importantly, music videos are easily shareable on social media and messaging apps such as Telegram, which is very popular in Iran. "This generation wants everything quick and in small bites," commented one producer, "so let's give them our own music videos." Since 2015, regime cultural producers have begun to pour more money and resources into producing music videos that they hope young people will not only consume but also make viral on Instagram and Telegram.

Mr. Hosseini believed that to attract young audiences, regime producers had to work with musicians popular among young people. He had been on a mission to reach out to rappers and rock bands who were popular with young audiences, while also trying to convince his colleagues that working with banned popular culture would pay off. He and his colleagues recruited Amir Tataloo, a thirty-two-year-old rapper with millions of followers on social media, who just the year before had been producing his music underground.[2] Tataloo had been arrested in December 2013 for his alleged cooperation with foreign satellite stations. Regime media producers recruited him to create a song about the nuclear issue. "Nuclear Energy" and the accompanying music video were released the day before the Iran nuclear deal was finalized on July 15, 2015. The music video took the Iranian cybersphere by storm because it features the rapper with Iran's military. Tataloo stands in front of actual members of the Iranian navy on a warship singing the chorus: "This is our absolute right, to have an armed Persian Gulf" (figure 2).

The video, with clear support from the regime and its military apparatus, shocked many Iranians, given that officials have snubbed rappers as westernized thugs at best and fomenters of evil at worst. The military's participation in a music video with an underground artist who flaunts his tattoos, long hair, and piercings, perplexed many Iranians. However, I had seen the Revolutionary Guard's media producers use this strategy since the rise of the Green Movement.

In the music video, Tataloo raps:

I'm not involved in political games. . . . /[But I know] if you are not being strong
and protecting your territory / then the smallest minds could penetrate. . . .
[What is needed is] something like a father for the family . . . /like a cop with a
baton for the thief / There needs to be protection for a bad day /a power to put
us ahead / *Chorus:* This is our absolute right, to have an armed Persian Gulf.

Most of the video takes place on the warship, but the material is intercut with
images of civilians holding signs in English, with messages such as "Has Iran
Ever Invaded a Country?"

Not only is the Persian Gulf an important symbol in this production, but
the song's emphasis on Iran's nuclear energy program is also key. Given the
experience of the 1953 coup d'état, Iran's ability to produce nuclear energy is
seen as a national right that must be defended. The reference to the Revolutionary Guard as the father of Iran is crucial in this music video. Using rap on
an Iranian warship in the Persian Gulf brings together all the symbols regime
media makers hoped to combine: the Revolutionary Guard, youth, and the
nation. The video attempts to rehabilitate the Revolutionary Guard for the nation, especially after the suppression of the Green Movement. Tataloo's video
is only the latest example of the ways in which the regime's cultural centers
have funded, supported, and promoted populist nationalism to attract young
audiences, often appropriating banned popular culture in the process.

The Howzeh Honari cultural center funded Iran's most expensive music
video to date, "We Are Standing until the Last Drop of Blood" (*Istādeh-im tā*

FIGURE 2. Screenshot from Amir Tataloo's "Nuclear Energy" music video.

ākharin Ghatreh-ye Khun; 2016), a seven-minute video that took over two years to make, using a 150-person crew, and cost USD 385,000 (figure 3). This video follows on the heels of the first "We Are Standing" (*Istādeh-im*) music video produced by Howzeh Honari and released on June 13, 2013, the day before the presidential elections. The Supreme Leader and those close to him were worried about voter turnout after the 2009 elections and the blow that the Green Movement had dealt to his legitimacy. This first music video, much less ambitious in production values than the second, shows a group of young male singers taking over Azadi (Freedom) Square. The musicians attract a large crowd and then begin to hand out flowers, miniature Iranian flags, juice boxes, and pictures of the Supreme Leader. The political purpose of the video—in the same square that young Green Movement protestors had inundated just four years prior demanding their votes to be counted—was to suggest (falsely) that there was mass youth support for the Supreme Leader. The music video played on state television for the election but got no traction on social media.

The second Howzeh Honari music video, "We Are Standing until the Last Drop of Blood," which made a greater impression due to its enormous budget by Iranian standards, was produced by the head of the center, Mohammad Reza Shefah.[3] The song tells the story of the downing of an Iran Air passenger flight by a U.S. ship in the Persian Gulf. Releasing the video in

FIGURE 3. "We Are Standing until the Last Drop of Blood" cover art.

September 2016 with great fanfare, Howzeh Honari staged a public viewing in its main Sureh Theater. An elaborate public relations campaign followed its release, including discussions on Iranian state television's leading arts programs.[4]

The music video starts with an Iran Air passenger plane taking off and flying over the southern border towns along the Persian Gulf. On the ground below, young boys play soccer on the beach, flanked by an oil refinery. Southern Bandari music, indigenous to the area, plays in the background, as if coming from someone's personal stereo. The video shows people going about their daily lives: outdoor cafes serve tea; fishermen are busy at work; women shop; painters work on a building and speak in the local Bandari accent; oil workers work at the refinery, speaking Tehrani-accented Persian; construction workers speak in local dialects; a couple has a picnic on the beach and watch their little daughter building sand castles; kids fly kites. In short, the idyllic Iranian imagined community of a multiethnic and multilingual country.

For the first three minutes of the video, there is no music as the viewer witnesses life unfold in this town. Then, when one of the boys from the beach soccer game runs into the water to get the soccer ball, an ominous shadow envelopes the beach and dark music begins to play. At this point, a missile rips into the Iran Air passenger plane and the boy's eyes fall on the U.S. naval warships, the source of the missile. Death, destruction, and chaos ensue. Women dressed in the region's distinctive clothing rush into the water to retrieve the dead. The singer, with a close-cut beard and scarf worn in the style of young Basiji men, emerges onto the beach, humming a melody as he walks defiantly toward the U.S. warships. As American fighter jets bomb the town, the singer and a group of multiethnic and multiracial Iranian men grab large Iranian flags, stand in unison, and march toward the U.S. warships.

"Like Kaveh's flag . . . I am the heir to Rostam, I am the master of Rakhsh" the singer bellows, making references to the *Shāhnāmeh*.[5] The connection between the historic defenders of the Persian world against foreign enemies and the warriors of the Islamic Republic is deliberate and clear. The song's lyrics make reference only to pre-Islamic Persian history, with no references at all to Islam, intentionally linking a particular understanding of the Persian past and the present.

When the U.S. warship fires a missile at the flag-bearing Iranian protectors, the men emerge from the debris and charge toward the water, brandishing Iranian flags as weapons. The Iranian flags create tremendous waves that turn on the warships, sinking them. The national flag is the only weapon the Basijis need against invaders. The USS *Vincennes*, the warship that in 1988 shot down Iran Air flight 655, killing all 290 people on board, is sunk in the music video.[6] In it, an American flag lies burning in the water, while the men with the Iranian flags kneel victoriously on one knee, looking at their conquest of the Persian Gulf, returning these waters to Iran.

These music videos were complemented by massive social media campaigns intending to lionize the Islamic Republic's warriors. Two social media campaigns in particular are meaningful examples of how the regime's media producers have attempted to recast the Revolutionary Guard. One is the campaign dedicated to Qassim Soleimani, the top commander of the Revolutionary Guard's elite Quds Special Forces. The second is the one dedicated to 175 Revolutionary Guard divers killed during the war with Iraq.

In 2015, Qassim Soleimani's division was responsible for extraterritorial and clandestine operations, which meant he was in charge of combatting ISIS and coordinating forces in Syria. He sprang onto the international scene, seemingly out of the blue. Soleimani is referred to as a "shadow" commander by Western journalists, stealthily fighting ISIS in Syria and Iraq on behalf of Iran.[7] News outlets and social media featured his familiar face as he posed for selfies on the frontlines, documentaries touted his military acumen, and music videos in Arabic passionately praised his strength and bravery.[8] The film studio Mostafa worked in was one of the regime production houses that participated in media campaigns about Soleimani.

The rapid advance of ISIS, a sworn enemy of Iran and Shiʿa Muslims, in the Middle East throughout 2014 and 2015 raised great alarm in Iran. The 2015 announcements in Iran that the country's intelligence services had uncovered plots to detonate bombs in Tehran created public frenzy.[9] To counter this atmosphere of fear about potential domestic terrorist attacks, regime cultural producers created social media campaigns, television pieces, films, and nationalist posters about the Revolutionary Guard, and Qassim Soleimani featured prominently in them.

"It's no joke what Haj Qassim [Soleimani] has been able to do. If it weren't for him, ISIS would have advanced throughout Iraq and would be at our doorstep. All Iranians owe him. We owe our safety to him, and I think our people are beginning to see that," Jafar, a twenty-seven-year old Basij filmmaker told me. One of Mostafa's colleagues and former classmates, Jafar was on one of the teams creating social media campaigns about Qassim Soleimani. These campaigns focused on two audiences: Arabs (mostly Iraqis, though also Lebanese and Syrians) and Iranians. Soleimani is branded in two ways: as a defender of the nation for Iranians and as the mastermind behind the fight against ISIS on the ground for both Arabs and Iranians. Due to this messaging, Soleimani as a figure is now adored not only by those who are pro–Islamic Republic but also, crucially, by those who view themselves as critical of the regime. Through these media campaigns, Soleimani is seen as a national hero defending Iran. He has been elevated above the factional politics of the state.

Documentaries, such as *Soleimani*, that paint Soleimani as the savior of Muslims in the face of fanatics are broadcast both in Persian and in Arabic and disseminated through YouTube, Telegram, Instagram, and Facebook channels on Shi'a politics. *Soleimani* starts with images of the commander and a song that bellows, "Hey, despicable enemy. I am Iranian. Do you think you intimidate us with your beheadings? We will not need to engage in a war with you as long as Qassim Soleimani is present." Made in the months after ISIS pushed closer to Iranian territory, the film touts Soleimani's role in training Iraqi fighters to defeat ISIS.

The surge in public displays of adoration for Soleimani are part of the larger public relations campaign by the Revolutionary Guard. Soleimani, or Haj Qassim, as he is affectionately known in Iran, became one of those heroes that regime media producers wanted to portray.

"At least the Revolutionary Guard keeps us safe. Look at what's happening all throughout the region. Bombs are going off everywhere, civil wars are unfolding, and Iran is the only stable country in the region," Golnaz, a twenty-two-year-old arts student at the University of Tehran, who is originally from Shiraz, told me during a ceremony that commemorated the dead who had been fighting in Syria. Since the rise of ISIS and the continued civil war in Syria, conversations among the third generation of the revolution, as they are known in Iran, or the 1990s generation (*dah-ye 70-ha*), had begun to change. In part, the change can be attributed to new regime media strategies. "I don't necessarily like them, but it's true what Golnaz says," her boyfriend, Kayvan, a film student, chimed in. "We're safe and living in a stable country thanks to them."

Around the same time, a second media campaign began. In June 2015, a state memorial service was held for 175 Iranian divers killed in Iraq during the bloody eight-year Iran-Iraq War. Large numbers of young men and women who do not usually attend regime rallies joined the event. Mostafa was one of the men involved in organizing the event. Events commemorating the war dead had been mainstays of the 1980s and 1990s in Iran. Like other regime events, mostly people who agreed with the system showed up to these ceremonies. But for this event, the organizers wanted something different.

Photos in Iranian media showed the 175 divers buried in their diving gear, their hands tied with wire. Shortly after they were discovered, it was decided that there would be a large public funeral for them in Tehran. "We wanted this public funeral to be different than the ones from over twenty years ago," Mr. Hosseini told me. "We knew we could make this a national issue." Production studios such as the one where Mostafa worked began to create a vast social media campaign for the divers. Memes on Instagram and Telegram featured the hashtag #theirhandsweretied. "We wanted to get across the idea that without these men dying for us, we wouldn't be an independent nation today," Mostafa said. "We're able to fight the likes of ISIS and stand up to the aggression of the Americans, Israelis, and Saudis in the region because our men fought so bravely for the whole country."

On the day of the public funeral, young people from the third generation came out in full force. It was unlike any regime event. "I'm here because I want to pay my respects to all those who have defended our nation," said Rosa, a twenty-two-year-old engineering student at the University of Tehran who describes herself as anti–Islamic Republic.

"It's not about the regime anymore," her boyfriend, Daryoush, added. "It's about the defense of Iran. Without these men who fought in that war, without leaders like Haj Qassim who are protecting Iran today, we'd be just like the other countries in our region."

"Look at how chaotic the entire region we live in is," said Sepideh, a twenty-six-year-old painter who is opposed to the regime. "Iran is the only stable, safe country in our region, and we have Qassim Soleimani and the Revolutionary Guard to thank for that."

The organizers of the memorial for the divers count that day as one of their most successful in reaching out to the "nonsupporters of the regime," as Mr. Hosseini explained to me. "We were able to bring them out because we've been successful in changing their minds about the Revolutionary Guard."

"Would our young men rise up and defend the country in the event of an attack? After 2009 we were afraid the answer was no. There was too much distrust and hatred against us for putting down that movement," Abbas, a Revolutionary Guard commander from Abadan said to me. "We needed to bring back this trust between us and the people, even the people who want reform in the system. It was crucial. And this public event proved that we could do it."

Conclusion

IN A STYLE TYPICAL OF STATE TELEVISION, a young interviewer stands on a sidewalk in a busy urban area and asks passersby their opinions about the recent protests across Iran in December 2017. A man in his sixties with tired eyes and heavy shoulders responds, "I have three kids. They're doctors and engineers. And all three are unemployed." A veteran of the Iran-Iraq War, surrounded by a crowd, defiantly tells the interviewer, "I need meds for my injuries from the war, but my medicine isn't covered and I'm told to go buy it on the black market. Who can afford that? I have a condition in my back and at any moment I could be paralyzed. Who am I supposed to go to for my pain?" In this high-production-value video by AvaNet TV, a new entity in Iran's sophisticated media landscape, a steady stream of people relay that they can no longer make ends meet in Iran's struggling economy.

The AvaNet TV video was released on social media five days after the start of the December 2017 protests in Iran, which spread across dozens of cities in almost all provinces.[1] It quickly went viral and was shared by activists, media outlets, and analysts both inside and outside Iran. The video carefully stitches together an array of emotional interviews with people speaking out against the economic situation and President Hassan Rouhani's policies. Because little public information is available about the new AvaNet TV internet television channel and its producers have taken great pains to present it as an independent station, the video appears to be a true representation of the will of the Iranian people. Glaringly absent are any criticisms of the political establishment as a whole, which had been one of the main reasons for the various demonstrations.

AvaNet TV is in fact not independent at all. It is only the latest example of a new Revolutionary Guard–backed media outlet that seeks to promote the narrative of the Supreme Leader in the politics of Iran. Like media outlets set up in the aftermath of the Green Movement, AvaNet TV points to the media wars at the heart of political factionalism both inside and outside Iran.

Regime media producers, following the large-scale protests in 2009, were cognizant that they faced a crisis of legitimacy. The director of one of the main channels of Islamic Republic of Iran Broadcasting told me in 2010, "We know we've lost a great deal of our audience to foreign satellite stations run by exiled Iranian communities. And our young people get their news and entertainment from social media outlets. State television is no longer the way. We need to figure out new ways to influence the narrative and bring the story back to our side."

The tactic that regime media producers developed in the aftermath of the 2009 protests was to move away from producing content solely for state television—which is almost automatically considered regime propaganda by potential audiences—to creating small production studios capable of generating content that is not easily identified as pro-regime. These ad hoc production studios receive funding from the Revolutionary Guard and the cultural budget of the government, yet they remain small and unidentifiable—on purpose. And because filmmakers are experimenting with different ways to make their media appealing to their audiences, their products are diverse and vary in their aesthetic choices, often making identifying them hard.

AvaNet TV began reaching the public on December 12, 2017, just days after President Rouhani revealed his budget for the next Iranian year (beginning in March) and publicly criticized "fraudulent institutions" for wreaking havoc on Iran's economy. In a speech to parliament about his proposed budget bill, Rouhani took specific aim at cultural institutions in the hands of hard-liners as well as long-standing funds allocated to clerics. In essence, he criticized some of the very media and cultural institutions that have been instrumental in lambasting the Green Movement as a foreign plot and in turn attacking Rouhani himself.

In revealing details of his new budget bill, Rouhani named, for the first time, the variety of state institutions—including cultural centers—that have received enormous funds and unconditional support from the regime with little oversight. He attributed the move to a desire for transparency and an attempt to curtail corruption. The reaction on Iranian social media and in the local press was quick and harsh: people began attacking conservative and hard-line centers and clerics for taking so much from the government's coffers.

"We couldn't allow him to cut off our lifeline," Mostafa said after Rouhani revealed his new budget. "He and his supporters want to silence us by taking away our funding. But we won't be silenced. We'll show him that people don't agree with him."

Much of the analysis of the sudden nationwide outpouring of protests in 2017-2018, the largest since the 2009 Green Movement, points to its origin in attempts to organize anti-Rouhani rallies in the lead-up to the annual pro-regime rally of 9 Dey, which had been created by the Supreme Leader in 2009 to celebrate the suppression of the Green Movement. Indeed, Mashhad, where the 2017-2018 protests began, is one of Iran's largest cities and notably is home to two of Rouhani's main rivals in the 2017 presidential elections. The December 2017 protests were supposed to culminate in the large annual rally to commemorate the suppression of the Green Movement on 9 Dey. However, despite the hard-liners' intentions to create a protest against Rouhani and his policies, once people came onto the streets, they began to chant slogans against the Supreme Leader and the regime as a whole.

Mostafa and his colleagues quickly realized that they could once again lose control of the narrative if the protest continued. Regime production studios have thus began to create videos that highlight economic anxieties and attack Rouhani's handling of the government. These slick new productions are meant to seem critical, but in the end, they reinforce a belief in the virtues and leadership of Ayatollah Ali Khamenei. AvaNet TV is only the latest example of the ways in which factionalism within the Islamic Republic and opposition to the regime play out in the Iranian mediascape.

The AvaNet TV video had been spread by activists and those frustrated by the regime and its economic policies. Yet, months later, when protests began to erupt once again because of the failing economy, the vast majority of slogans were not about President Rouhani and his policies but about corruption at the highest echelons of power, the Supreme Leader, and the system as a whole. Once again, regime media makers fretted about their loss of control over the narrative.

In less than a decade, from the suppression of the 2009 Green Movement to the rise of ISIS and then of new national protests against economic mismanagement and rampant corruption, regime media producers went from anxious meetings about their relationship with young audiences to celebrating their successes to becoming anxious yet again. The work of messaging ideology and defending a revolutionary project to a population is never-ending—especially when simultaneous efforts are under way by foreign powers and opposition groups to provide counternarratives via satellite television and radio stations, news websites, and social media. In the end, it's a media war that is intended to question the very legitimacy of the Islamic Republic. To defend that legitimacy, Iran's military and paramilitary forces continue to pour money into this fight.

Yet, even internally, regime media makers do not all agree on the "right" path to take. The question at the very heart of these debates is how to define the regime and what it stands for today. Deciding how to tell the stories of a revolutionary project entails difficult conversations about which stories to tell, whose stories are included, and how to frame the issues at hand. The revolutionary zeal of the founding decades is now gone, and regime media producers face the dilemma of how to replace it with a commitment to the regime in the face of fierce international pressure. To make matters even more complicated, regime media producers in Iran have to contend with the fact that audiences dismiss anything they produce as propaganda. So how do they get a message across when a large portion of the audience no longer wants to engage?

In the Islamic Republic, a revolutionary system has become the status quo, and now the Republic faces the question of how to keep its system "alive." This question entails two main challenges: how to safeguard the socioeconomic and class status of its leaders and how to appeal to younger generations and their demands for political participation. The solutions that regime media producers have offered in Iran are threefold: to hide the origins of regime discourse through strategies of dissimulation, to create new distribution strategies, and to appeal to notions of nationalism as a unifying force beyond political ideology, especially in the face of growing sectarianism in the region, proxy wars with Saudi Arabia, and an understanding that Iran's youth is no longer motivated by political Islam.

As I have shown, these strategies have met with some success. Regime cultural producers across the political and generational spectrums, from Mr. Hosseini and Mr. Ahmadi to Mostafa, unanimously agreed on the success of the campaign surrounding Qassim Soleimani and the public funeral for the 175 divers. "We're finally beginning to see the results of our efforts," Mr. Hosseini said with a big smile on his face after that event. Mostafa, too, who had originally dismissed Mr. Hosseini's plea to engage strategically with gheyr-e khodis, had worked hard on the divers' funeral and was pleased. Yet, with continued protests against the regime, especially in regard to corruption and continued social repression, anxieties about needing to create new strategies have started again.

Crucially though, the question of how to manage media narratives is not exclusive to Iran, or even to revolutionary states. With the vast advances in media technology—including the fact that smartphones are now easily accessible to many people—states, media companies, and citizens the world over struggle to understand the terrain of this new media sphere and how it affects politics. Anxieties over media technology and politics are not new.[2] However, the ease with which news and stories travel today and the ways in which states, corporations, and organizations can manipulate digital media to promote certain stories and political objectives over others have made examining the intersection of media and politics even more crucial—and complicated.

Iran Reframed has attempted to look at this intersection from the point of view of those in power in Iran. As Mr. Hosseini told me after nationwide protests erupted once again in Iran in 2018,

> We're in a never-ending project. We tell our stories as best we can, and some-
> times we do it well. But we're dealing with a generation that prefers to get all

their information from their phones. Look, I've told you many times these past ten years that we've had our share of big mistakes. We've censored voices and made people distrust us. But we're also dealing with a situation in which powerful states are against us and are pouring money into media that our population consumes to make them hate us even more. I don't know if anyone has figured out how to solve this problem. And it's not just a problem that we face in Iran.

Mr. Hosseini continues to travel around the country and world to promote films that he has helped make to tell the story of the Iran-Iraq War. His daughters, now adults, both work as professionals, and one of them wishes to continue her studies in Europe. They want to have nothing to do with politics or the past. When I asked him if it bothers him that his daughters have not decided to follow his path in defending the stories of the war or the revolution, he shrugs with a resigned smile on his face: "All they have heard since they were born was me talking about the war. They want to make their own life now."

Mr. Ahmadi's daughter is an emerging art photographer who has begun to exhibit not just in Iran but in Europe as well. Her work, notably, has nothing to do with the war or the revolution either. Instead, her artwork deals with the female body and who wields control over it. Although her father has vast connections in the regime media world, she has decided not to engage with that world at all and instead try to make it as an independent artist.

Mr. Ahmadi's son has decided to follow his father's path and become a cultural producer in a regime institution. But his son's wife often asked me for information about how they could get a visa to leave Iran. As the daughter of a wounded veteran, as well as being from a pious family that supported the regime, she was a surprising candidate for emigration. I asked her why she would want to leave her life in Iran if she and her family had fared so well financially and were connected to the state. She gave me a knowing look with a smile: "It's suffocating to be surrounded by all this talk of politics all the time. My husband and I want to give our son a different world, but we can't here. My husband pretends that he likes what he's doing, following in the footsteps of his father, but he's also looking for a way out for us. It breaks our family's heart for them to hear we want to leave, but there's no place for us here."

I asked Mostafa if he still stood by his beliefs from his days as the head of his university Basij association and the leader of the Art Circle. "Ever since my daughter was born," he explained to me, "I've noticed a shift. I lie awake at night thinking about the kind of country she's going to grow up in. I don't want her to have the difficulties I've had in school with kids who weren't like me. I want her to grow up happy and surrounded by friends and able to do whatever she wants."

He paused for some time before continuing, "So in that way, I guess I've changed. But I know she'll be safe and can grow up in an independent country"—he looked at me and made eye contact—"because our military forces will defend us. So, in that way my beliefs haven't changed. But now I do agree that if we're really going to defeat all these forces that are out to get us, we need to be unified as a country."

By taking the lived experiences of those who work on behalf of the regime in Iran seriously and understanding why they continue to fight to uphold a system they have qualms about from time to time, we can see these men as complex actors who work beyond the binary that often dominates political talk in Iran (reformist versus hard-liner; anti-regime versus pro-regime). This exercise requires us to see that regime media producers have fierce debates with one another about the future of the country, to understand that they are constantly challenged and changed by their children, to recognize that they struggle among themselves to define what the future of the Islamic Republic will look like, and to observe how they use both formal and informal channels of power to demarcate what is and is not allowed. Contestation in the Islamic Republic is not just between the regime and the people or between the older generations and the young. Instead, by focusing an ethnographic lens on those who work to advance the regime, this research reveals a multilayered story that complicates existing understandings of what it means to be "pro-regime" in the Islamic Republic.

Acknowledgments

This project would not have been possible without the help and support of so many beautiful and kind individuals. To my interlocutors in Iran, who guided my research and opened doors, I can never thank you enough. Many of them cannot be named here, and for others, I have used pseudonyms, but I hope they recognize their stories in this work and I hope I have done justice to their struggles and aspirations. To the man I name Mr. Hosseini, I could not have done this research without him. From the bottom of my heart, I thank him for his guidance and his belief in my project. To SK, the man who first introduced me to the world of war veterans and chemical weapons survivors, I extend my utmost gratitude and appreciation. He allowed me to witness the stories of survival and helped me dive deeper into understanding the horrors of war. To MT, my sincere thanks for looking out for me during the filming of my documentary and during the research. I know he vouched for me multiple times with various security forces and made sure I did not get in trouble. I can never thank him enough for his trust, his open heart, and his desire to ensure that silenced voices from his war generation are heard.

I am beyond blessed to have the most supportive and caring mentors a young scholar can hope for. Faye Ginsburg has made New York University's Anthropology Department the best place on earth to study and learn about media and media practitioners. She not only provided a supportive environment for me to learn and thrive, but she taught me through example what it means to be an incisive yet generous scholar and a gracious mentor. I hope to one day be able to give to my future students a fraction of the care and insight she offered to me. I can also never thank her enough for standing by me and my project when I ran into legal issues due to the Iran sanctions. She was at every meeting and stood by my side during a rough ride.

To Bruce Grant, I owe an ocean's worth of gratitude. The hours I spent in his office talking about my project and trying to figure out what I wanted to say were invaluable to me. He taught me how to formulate my half-baked ideas into worthy questions and lines of inquiry. Bruce walked me through the nuts of bolts of academia and showed me how to get through each step. I am beyond lucky to have had such generous guidance.

I thank Bambi Schieffelin for opening up the world of linguistic anthropology and teaching me how not only to pay close attention to what is said but to look just as closely for what is not said. Working in an environment surrounded by military elite in Iran, this guidance and advice was valuable. Her office remains one of my favorite spots in New York to be because I know I will be listened to deeply. Bambi is the best person to brainstorm with, and I always leave her office with a hundred new ideas and avenues to explore. Her love and care for her students is legendary, and I count myself lucky to have received it.

I could not think of a better scholar than Arang Keshavarzian to learn from about the intricacies of contemporary Iran and to exchange ideas with about research in Tehran. He is an amazing political scientist who understands and values ethnography, and he was instrumental in helping me figure out how to bring an anthropological eye to questions of the state and power. He never failed to encourage me and to push me to think more critically about my research. I especially thank him for constantly reminding me to keep an open mind about my work and to push past partisanship.

Hamid Naficy believed in my project and in my ability to carry it out even before I embarked on it. His pioneering scholarship on media in Iran has opened up exciting spaces of inquiry for several generations of scholars researching Iran and media. My work and thinking are deeply indebted to his scholarship, and I am grateful for his encouragement and keen insight since I first sat in his office in Evanston in 2007.

I have long admired Michael Gilsenan's pioneering scholarship on the Middle East, and I count myself lucky to have had wonderful conversations with him on the Middle East, masculinity, violence, anthropology, and Islam. I will always treasure our lunches in the West Village.

Thank you to all the marvelous scholars who taught me anthropology in New York: Thomas Abercrombie, Sonia Das, Tejaswini Ganti, Emily Martin, Sally Merry, Fred Myers, Susan Rogers, Leslie Sharp, Noelle Stout, and Angela Zito. To Fred Ritchin and Susan Measles at NYU Tisch and the Magnum Foundation, thank you for eye-opening conversations and the push to always think more critically about representation. In the crazy world that is New York, a space to think and write is as valuable as gold, and I thank Noelle Stout for lending me her office and for being so generous outside the classroom.

I thank Noelle Stout once more, as well as Cheryl Furjanic and Marco Williams for teaching me the magic of filmmaking and for instilling in me a love for visual storytelling.

A tremendous amount of gratitude goes to Daniel Magida, general counsel at NYU, who walked me through nine months of legal issues with the U.S. Department of Treasury, and did so with great kindness. My research, quite literally, would not have been possible without his hard work and guidance.

And thanks to all my colleagues and students at the Watson Institute at Brown University and at the School of Advanced International Studies, Johns Hopkins University. I couldn't have asked for better institutions to be at while I wrote this book. A special thank-you to Julia Vich-Bertran, Gregory Morton, and Lindsey Reynolds, who read every word of this manuscript multiple times and offered crucial feedback. Beyond their sharp minds, I am lucky to count them as my friends. No amount of thank-yous would suffice for the type of mentorship, feedback, and friendship Sherine Hamdy has offered. I thank her for encouraging me to write this book with my own voice. A special thank-you to Sherine, Amahl Bishara, and Ilana Feldman, who, along with Parsa Bastani and Samee Sulaiman, read an earlier version of this book and provided invaluable feedback. To Sarah Besky, Keith Brown, Bishara Doumani, Cathy Lutz, thank you for all your guidance. To my students at Brown, you all taught me more than you know with your incisive questions and desire for critical knowledge. Thank you for making a teacher out of me and for helping me find my voice. I cherish each and every one of you.

Academia can often be a cold, hard place. But fellow colleagues offered extraordinary friendship and camaraderie every step of the way: Dwai Banajeree, Nicholas Barnes, Giuliana Borea, Matthew Canfield, Robert Chang, Ernesto de Carvalho, Lee Douglas, Amy Field, Jennifer Greenberg, Amali Ibrahim, Michelle Jurkovich, Mohammad Ali Kadivar, Rachel Lears, Tate LeFevre, Irina Levin, Rahul Mediratta, Almita Miranda, Amir Moosavi, Gregory Morton, Hyejin Nah, Vijyanka Nair, Ram Natarajan, Yusuf Neggers, Wazhmah Osman, Anthony Pratcher II, Rowena Potts, Louis Romer, Stephanie Sadre-Orfai, Aarti Sethi, Perry Sherouse, Elena Shih, Leili Sreberny-Mohammadi, Lucas Stanczyk, Adaner Usmani, Elizabeth Williams, and Tyler Zoanni. A very special thanks to Yasmin Moll, who allowed me to learn from her many, many successes—I could not have come as far as I have without her generosity and mentoring every step of the way. Rowena Potts and Cheryl Furjanic represent all that is good about academia. They improved my spirits daily, whether in New York City or via WhatsApp. Their friendship sustained me through all the ups and downs. To my "digital doreh," thank you for your friendship, advice, and amazing memes and laughter when it was most needed: Beeta Bagholizadeh, Sarah Khanghahi, Neda Maghbouleh, and Amy Malek.

Thank you to Orkideh Behrouzan, Hamid Dabashi, Michael Fischer, Kim Fortun, Behrooz Ghamari-Tabrizi, Kevan Harris, Mazyar Lotfalian, Amy Malek, Shervin Malekzadeh, Ali Mirsepassi, Amir Moosavi, Negar Mottahedeh, Nahid Mozaffari, Afsaneh Najmabadi, Nasrin Rahmanian, Negar Razavi, and Naghmeh Sohrabi for their conversations, incisive questions, and scholarship, which informed my work and pushed me to explore my questions more deeply.

I am also thankful to the SSRC-IDRF workshop in 2015, most especially Richard Wittman and Kris Manjapra; their encouragement and comments came at a crucial time in this work. Thank you to my fellow participants in that workshop—Nicolas Barnes, Teofilo Ballve, Ariel Bize Melnick, Maura Capps, Robyn d'Avignon, Elizabeth Dyer, Ian Goldstein, Aubrey Graham, and Delia Wendel—for inspiring me to continue writing.

Because I am a first-generation immigrant and the eldest child in my family, my teachers played an immense role in opening possibilities and helping me navigate an American system alien to my family. There are too many to name here, but each of them has had a profound impact on my life, in all stages of my education. But two of my professors at Wellesley College, in particular, exposed me to critical thought and the power of the social sciences, and they gave me the tools to question long-standing assumptions with care and diligence. I thank Roxanne Euben and Katharine Moon for everything they taught me and for modeling what it means to be an academic. I am so lucky to have been taught by the two of them at such a young age. A huge thank-you goes too to Amahl Bishara, who exposed me to anthropology at the University of Chicago and made me a convert.

Since childhood, I have been inspired by family friends in Iran, who I consider my chosen family—by their bravery, unending fight for justice, belief in humankind, activism, and perseverance in the face of the toughest obstacles of imprisonment, torture, and loss. Even though I have written about the very institutions and men they have spent the last four decades fighting, they have encouraged me every step of the way, have pushed me to ask the tough questions, and have taught me to never forget those who have been silenced by power. I can never thank them enough. To my friends, family, and colleagues in Iran who not only encouraged me but listened intently, offered constructive criticism, and most importantly nurtured me with their kindness and hospitality, thank you. I won't name them for many reasons, but they know who they are.

To my family and friends in New York, Virginia, and beyond who sustained me the past decade with their love, made me laugh, enjoy life, and dance, I love you dearly: Taghi Amirani, Nassim Assefi, Arash Azizzada, Rahim Bajoghli, Alireza Ehteshami, Parisa Elahi, Ellie Etedali, Shervin Etemad, Kayvan Farchadi, Bijan Farnoudi, Shirin Hakimzadeh, Ali Hirsa, Bahman Kalbasi, Mana Kharrazi, Amy Malek, Jana Marini, Kiesha Minyard, Golnaz Moazami, Ali Moazami, Tanaz Moazami, Behrooz Moazami, Jilla Moazami, Mahbubeh Mozayan, Nahid Navab, Nasrin Navab, Naser Navab, Elahe Nezhadhosseini, Abdol Ostad, Ramin Ostad, Rasa Ostad, Lily Panah, Mani Parcham, Nikoo Paydar, Laura Pena, Nhan Pho, Pari Pooladi, Leyla Pope,

Aida Sadr-Kiani, Diana Sands, Fereshteh Sani, Zohreh Sepehr, Leyla Serway, Afsoon Talai, and Pablo Trincia.

A lifetime of appreciation and thanks to my brother, Ramin, for being the most supportive person in the world, for always having my back, and for always reminding me not to take myself too seriously. I love you to the moon and back.

To my grandmother, Fatemeh Moazami, who sadly passed away right before I began this research, my gratitude and love is infinite. Living with her in her magical house in Tehran all throughout my twenties was the best decision I ever made. She is the one who taught me to listen to and respect everyone's stories, especially those with whom I disagree. She was the strongest woman I have ever met, and her stories and lessons are ever present, as if she recounted them to me just yesterday over tea. Her memory lives on and I hope she is proud of what became of this research.

To my parents, Javad Bajoghli and Mahla Moazami, there are no words that could capture my immense gratitude and love. They raised me on a healthy dose of stories of resistance and shared humanity, and they helped me understand that the struggle for a just society is a long and difficult one. My father is the biggest feminist I know, my number-one fan, and my confidant. I could never have embarked on this project without his encouragement— every time I was afraid to continue, he pushed me back out on the street and taught me that I have nothing to fear. No matter how frustrated I was or what a difficult day I was having, the unconditional love of my amazingly loving mother made everything okay again. She has always been a source of calm and strength. Thank you both for your sacrifices and never-ending encouragement.

A tremendous amount of love and gratitude to my best friend, husband, and partner-in-crime, Gerardo Contino, for being so supportive through all the long-distance research and for filling my life with music. I am especially indebted to him for making sure I have a full and fun life outside my work, filled with immense love. And to our lovely little Leyla, who has filled our world with so much light. I wrote the book while pregnant with her, and rewrote it while learning to be a parent. She has made it all worthwhile and has filled our lives with more love than I ever thought possible. A special thanks to all of her amazing caretakers at her daycare; without them, I could never have finished this book.

Several centers and institutes provided their support at different stages of the project: the Social Science Research Council, the Wenner-Gren Foundation for Anthropological Research, and the American Institute for Iranian Studies have funded fieldwork in Iran for this research. An NYU Dean's Fellowship and the NYU Center for the Humanities supported the earlier writing of this study. I also gratefully acknowledge the generous financial support provided by NYU's MacCracken and Torch Fellowships, as well as the Wellesley College Alice Palmer Fellowship. Thank you to colleagues at Princeton University, Boston University, Brown University, Duke University, Northwestern University, and New York University for their critical feedback at various workshops where I presented this work.

To Susan Frekko, who read this manuscript with such care, offered thoughtful feedback and edits, and helped transform it, thank you. At Stanford University Press, I want to especially thank Kate Wahl. I couldn't have asked for a better editor with a sharper eye. Thank you for your guidance in pulling this together, and for giving me the green light to write this book as I wanted to write it, not how it "should" be.

Notes

Preface

1. For more on Dehnamaki's films, please see Bajoghli, 2017, "*The Outcasts.*"

Introduction

1. I have changed the names of most of my interlocutors in order to protect their identities. When interlocutors requested it, I additionally changed other identifying details, such as the name of the city they come from (though I replaced it with a city in the same geographic area). I have not changed the names of the filmmakers when I write about their work. Although I have translated the conversations, interviews, meetings, and films that appear in this book from Persian to English, I have done my best to capture the language with which each person spoke.

2. Given that Iran's elections use paper ballots, several days usually pass before the counts are complete and the results are announced.

3. Transliteration of Persian words is done in accordance with Iranian Studies Association.

4. Throughout my research, my interlocutors referred to the media they produced in the 1980s and 1990s as "propaganda" (using the English word, not the Persian word *tabliqāt*). As has been widely discussed, the word *propaganda*, beyond offering a general sense of "manipulation," is an incredibly difficult word to define, as it tends to depend on one's perspective. In this book, I use it only if an interlocutor uses the word. For more in-depth discussion of propaganda, please see, among others, Stanley, 2015, *How Propaganda Works*; Taylor, 2003, *Munitions of the Mind*; Ellul, 1973, *Propaganda: The Formation of Men's Attitudes*.

5. There has been much debate among scholars about usage of *fundamentalist* to describe Islamists, given the category's Protestant roots. For more discussion on this in the context of Ayatollah Khomeini and the Islamic Republic, please see Abrahamian, 1993, *Khomeinism*.

6. Bajoghli, 2014, "Digital Media as Surveillance."

7. For a more in-depth discussion of research in national security environments, please see Bajoghli, forthcoming, "The Researcher as National Security Threat."

8. Deeb and Winegar, 2015, *Anthropology's Politics*.

9. For more on the concept of "media worlds," see Ginsburg, Abu-Lughod, and Larkin, 2002, *Media Worlds*.

Chapter 1: Generational Changes

1. Avini, the most prolific filmmaker of the Iran-Iraq War, produced over twenty-five documentaries from the frontlines of the war, seventeen of which were series that were broadcast weekly on national television, bringing the total number of episodes to 167. After the end of the war in 1988 until July 1992, Avini was the chief editor of *Sureh* magazine, published by Howzeh Honari. Approximately sixteen books have been published posthumously based on his written works, articles, and film narrations.

Avini graduated from Hadaf High School, one of the most prestigious high schools in Tehran, in 1965 and attended the Fine Arts Faculty of Tehran University, graduating with a master's degree in architecture. After the 1979 Revolution, Avini joined the Reconstruction Campaign (Jahad-e Sāzandegi), traveling to underserved villages and towns to meet basic needs. In this campaign, he became a member of the television crew, and when one of his colleagues, Hossein Hashemi, was taken as a prisoner of war by the Iraqi forces on the battlefront of the new war, Avini decided to turn his attention to documenting the war.

2. For more on the 1979 Revolution, please see Abrahamian, 2009, *A History of Modern Iran*; Arjomand, 1986, "Iran's Islamic Revolution in Comparative Perspective"; Bayat, 2007, *Street Politics*; Dabashi, 2007a, *Iran: A People Interrupted*; Farhi, 1990, *State and Urban-Based Revolution: Iran and Nicaragua*; Fischer, 2003, *Iran: From Religious Dispute to Revolution*; Kazemi, 1980, *Poverty and Revolution in Iran*; Keddie, 2003, *Modern Iran: Roots and Results of Revolution*; Kurzman, 2004, *The Unthinkable Revolution in Iran*; Moaddel, 1992, *Class, Politics, and Ideology in the Iranian Revolution*; Mottahedeh, 1985, *The Mantle of the Prophet*; Paidar, 1995, *Women and the Political Process in 20th-Century Iran*; Parsa, 1989, *Social Origins of the Iranian Revolution*; Skocpol, 1982, "Rentier State and Shi' a Islam in the Iranian Revolution."

3. On state television, it is not uncommon to see images of the revolution with certain figures who became critics of the Islamic Republic photoshopped out of them.

4. Abrahamian, 1993, *Khomeinism*, 26.

5. In 1912, the Anglo-Persian Oil Company (later British Petroleum, and then BP) completed the Abadan refinery, one of the world's largest oil refineries. It controlled the refinery until Iranian Prime Minister Mohammad Mossadegh nationalized the oil industry in 1951. The Americans and British regained control of the oil industry in the country after an orchestrated coup d'état in 1953 that reinstated the Shah and turned him into the biggest ally of the United States in the Middle East. By the time of the revolution, Abadan was a cosmopolitan international city and the hub of the National Iranian Oil Company. For more, see Abrahamian, 2013, *The Coup: 1953, the CIA, and the Roots of Modern U.S.-Iranian Relations*.

6. Ostovar, 2016, *Vanguard of the Imam*.

7. Chubin and Tripp, 1988, *Iran and Iraq at War*, 33.

8. To read more on class and the revolutionary period, please see Amir-Arjomand, 1986, "Iran's Islamic Revolution in Comparative Perspective"; Farhi, 1990, *State and Urban-Based Revolution: Iran and Nicaragua*; Harris, 2017, *A Social Revolution: Politics and the Welfare State in Iran*; Kazemi, 1980, *Poverty and Revolution in Iran*; Kurzman, 2004, *The Unthinkable Revolution in Iran*; Moaddel, 1992, *Class, Politics, and Ideology in the Iranian Revolution*; Parsa, 1989, *Social Origins of the Iranian Revolution*; Skocpol, 1982, "Rentier State and Shi' a Islam in the Iranian Revolution."

9. Personal interviews.

10. Calculated using 1986 USD-to-rial conversion rates (U.S. Department of Treasury, Treasury Reporting Rates of Exchange, as of March 31, 1986, https://fiscal.treasury.gov/reports-statements/treasury-reporting-rates-exchange/).

11. For more on generations in postrevolutionary Iran, see Behrouzan, 2016, *Prozak Diaries: Psychiatry and Generational Memory in Iran*.

12. Khomeini, 1989, "Last Will and Testament," 45.

13. Golkar, 2012, "Paramilitarization of the Economy."

14. Since the end of the war, the Revolutionary Guard has launched numerous companies and has received lucrative government contracts. Unlike other enterprises, the Revolutionary Guard does not report its income to the Central Bank, and thus its net value is unknown. The Revolutionary Guard's companies receive multibillion-dollar contracts from the government, yet because they often lack the technical know-how to execute many of the projects, they outsource the work. These Guard-owned and -operated businesses are active in such industries as oil, agriculture, road and dam construction, and automobile manufacturing. For example, the Revolutionary Guard-owned Bahman Group has a monopoly on assembling Mazda cars in Iran.

One of the most lucrative Revolutionary Guard–owned enterprises is Khatam al-Anbia, an energy firm that was awarded the development of phases 15 and 16 of the South Pars gas fields in June 2006. This contract, along with the contract for the offshore development of the site, is valued at $9.2 billion. The following year, Khatam al-Anbia was awarded a $3.1 billion contract to construct the major pipeline connecting Asaluyeh (in southern Iran) to the Sistan and Baluchistan Province.

In the area of transportation, the Revolutionary Guard–owned National Company of Construction and the Foundation for the Oppressed were awarded $2.4 billion in June 2006, with the Tehran Metro Company, to work on further expanding the Tehran metro. And perhaps most importantly, in July 2007, the Ministry of Energy stated that Revolutionary Guard contractors would operate all public infrastructure projects involving water, electricity, and bridges in western Iran. Many of these contracts were (and continue to be) awarded on a no-bid basis, in violation of Iranian law, which mandates open bidding.

In addition to its contracts, the Revolutionary Guard also operates its own "free-trade ports," where the average Iranian businessman who wants to import or export items is subject to heavy tariffs. The Revolutionary Guard itself, because it runs the ports, is not subject to tariffs. Thus, the Revolutionary Guard has strategically placed itself in key economic positions within the country and has gained considerable clout because of its business dealings.

15. Classes included *velayat* (guardianship) in 1997, *basirat* (insight) in 1998, and *marefat* (awareness) in 2001. For more, see Golkar, 2010a, "The Ideological-Political Training of Iran's Basij."

16. Golkar, 2010a.

17. To read more about the origins of soft war discourse and its history in Iran, see Sabet and Safshekan, 2013, *Soft War*.

18. The Supreme Leader's idea that media can "vaccinate" audience members from harmful ideas resonates with early Western media theory (beginning in the 1920s into the 1930s), sometimes known as the hypodermic needle theory—that is, a linear model suggesting that media simply injects material into the minds of passive audiences, and they will accept the intended message. This theory of media emerged after Western researchers—Harold Lasswell in particular (1927)—observed the effect of propaganda during World War I. It was later rejected as overly simplified in the work of early communications scholars, such as the sociologist Paul Lazarsfeld, in the 1940s.

In the lead-up to the 1979 Revolution in Iran, anticinema feelings ran deep, particularly among the religious strata. As Hamid Naficy explores in *The Islamicate Period 1978–1984*, vol. 3 of *A Social History of Iranian Cinema* (2012), the clerical elite subscribed to this hypodermic theory of media and ideology. Throughout the twentieth century in Iran, clerical elites decried cinema for its "corrupting" values, especially given the depiction of unveiled women, dancing, drinking, and gambling prominent in films produced during the Pahlavi reign. Ayatollah Khomeini used the term *injection* (*tazriq*) to describe the direct effects of Western-propagated culture, including media and cinema. In his book *Velayat-e Faqih* (*Rule of Jurisprudence*; 1981), which outlines the framework for the future Islamic Republic, Khomeini writes about cinema as the direct cause of prostitution, corruption, and political dependence on the West.

Importantly, however, Khomeini and his cohort of revolutionary clerics did not ban cinema after the Shah was ousted; instead, they called for a reformed cinema and entertainment industry that reflected the values of the new revolutionary state. In his first speech back in Iran following the triumph of the revolution, Ayatollah Khomeini, in front of thousands at Tehran's large Behesht-e Zahra cemetery, stated, "We are not opposed to cinema, to radio, or to television. . . . The cinema is a modern invention that ought to be used for the sake of educating the people, but as you know, it was used instead to corrupt our youth. It is the misuse of cinema that we are opposed to, a misuse caused by the treacherous policies of our rulers" (1981, 258).

After the death of Khomeini, the new Supreme Leader, Ayatollah Khamenei, continued in this line and stated that the West "injected" its corrupting culture into Iran "not with a hypodermic needle, but with radio and television, fashion magazines, advertising, and ballyhoo" (1994, 17). Naficy argues: "Injection theory would soon become part of the new regime's counteroffensive against Western cultural invasion and imperialism" (2012, 3:6). Nonetheless, Iranian filmmakers from all political stripes have a sophisticated practical sense of the efficacy of media, while some, like Mr. Hosseini, have a sophisticated discursive sense that undergirds the remarkable social experiments they engage in, such as the meeting between pro-regime cultural critics and independent filmmakers discussed earlier in the chapter.

19. Golkar, 2015, *Captive Society*.

20. For more information, please see the Soft War and Psychological Operations website (in Persian): http://www.swar.ir/about.aspx.

21. In the same vein, the Supreme Leader has waged a defense against the soft war by calling for the restructuring of Iran's universities to include indigenous (that is, Islamic) social sciences and indigenous Islamic culture via films and televisions serials (*boomi-saazi*). These initiatives are informed by real threats from the point of view of the Islamic Republic: with U.S. forces on all of Iran's borders, the Islamic Republic's armed forces are in a constant state of vigilance; cyberattacks by the U.S. and Israel on Iran have caused severe damage (Zetter, 2014, *Countdown to Zero Day*); Iranian nuclear scientists have been assassinated both in Iran and abroad; international actors have financially supported, and at times trained, Iran's ethnic minorities to incite rebellion; and sections of the Iranian diaspora have waged constant media war against the Islamic Republic, including some stations that are funded by Western countries and Israel.

22. Nasrabadi, forthcoming, *Neither Washington, Nor Tehran*.

23. Personal interviews.

24. For more on the creation of an exilic culture via television, please see Naficy, 2001a, *An Accented Cinema*.

25. Akhavan, 2015, *Electronic Iran: The Cultural Politics of an Online Evolution*; Alavi, 2006, *We Are Iran*; Kamalipour, 2010, *Media, Power, and Politics in the Digital Age*; Sreberny and Khiabany, 2010, *Blogistan: The Internet and Politics in Iran*.

26. Emad Khazraee, an assistant professor at Kent State University, is currently researching this topic.

27. Interviews with the author, Tehran 2010–2013.

28. Some of their children had Basij cards to be able to go on school trips, but none were active members.

Chapter 2: Cracks in the Official Story

1. Since the regime had come under intense internal pressure following the treatment of prisoners from the Green Movement protests—including accusations of severe beatings, rape, and executions—pro-regime cultural centers needed a way to deflect the criticism. What made these accusations different from those in the previous three decades was that some of the people speaking the loudest this time about the treatment of prisoners were themselves part of the regime. Their children had been rounded up while protesting and had been beaten and, in some instances, raped. Attempting to cast a shadow on the accusations, the Supreme Leader's Office created this new initiative to publish stories of Iraqis held in Iranian prisons during the war to illustrate how "benign" and "humanitarian" Iranian prisons were for the Iraqi soldiers, as one of the speakers at the event had said.

2. For more on the role of *bonyāds* (foundations) in Iran, see Harris, 2017, *A Social Revolution: Politics and the Welfare State in Iran*.

3. To read more about acting "as if" in spaces of authoritarian power, see Wedeen, (1999) 2015, *Ambiguities of Domination*.

4. Deer, 2009, *Culture in Camouflage*.

5. For more on the development of war culture in Iran, see Moosavi, 2015, "Dust That Never Settled"; Naficy, 2012, *The Islamicate Period*, vol. 3 of *A Social History of Iranian Cinema*; Rastegar, 2015, *Surviving Images: Cinema, War, and Cultural Memory in the Middle East*; Zeydabadi-Nejad, 2009, *The Politics of Iranian Cinema*.

6. Avini, 1996, Farabi, 33–34.

Chapter 3: Insiders, Outsiders, and Belonging

1. For more on the complex web of publishing in Iran, see *Writer's Block: The Story of Censorship in Iran*, 2015, Small Media, www.smallmedia.org.uk/writersblock /file/Writer'sBlock.pdf.

2. *Kayhan* is one of Iran's most hard-line newspapers, headed by Hossein Shari-atmadari, a top advisor to the Supreme Leader. Both Tasnim News Agency and *RajaNews* are hard-line outlets, and Fars News Agency is Iran's most hard-line news agency, known to be loyal to the Supreme Leader.

3. In Islam, it is not permissible for women and men who are not related in specific ways to touch. Thus, only women and men who are *mahram* to one another are able to touch. *Mahram* is defined as "unmarriageable kin with whom intercourse would be considered incestuous." Thus, a man's wife, mother, sisters, daughters, granddaughters, nieces, mother-in-law, and sisters-in-law are mahram. In contemporary Iran, in certain settings, non-mahram (*nāmahram*) men and women will shake hands. But in more pious settings or government settings, shaking hands is still taboo.

4. The Farabi Cinema Foundation was established in 1983, and it is involved in a wide variety of work in relation to Iranian cinema. Primarily, Farabi produces films, gives low-rate loans, supplies raw materials, lends camera equipment, provides postproduction facilities, and sponsors film festivals. It is also responsible for promoting and marketing Iranian cinema internationally.

5. Although officially the prisoners were deemed "counterrevolutionary," protests of the rampant extrajudicial killings date back to the first decade of the revolution, with such high-profile clerics as Grand Ayatollah Montazeri writing letters of protest to Ayatollah Khomeini, condemning the executions. Due to these letters of protest, Khomeini demoted Montazeri, who had been favored to become his successor, and chose Ali Khamenei as Supreme Leader instead.

6. As long as gheyr-e khodis act as the normal other onto which the values of the system can be projected and juxtaposed, they do not threaten the system because the possibility of reforming these "others" into "good revolutionaries" is always present. The system needs the gheyr-e khodi to define itself against. For more on how the outsider is needed in revolutionary contexts, see Buck-Morss, 2002, *Dreamworld and Catastrophe*.

7. In the decades leading up to the Iranian revolution of 1979, khodi and gheyr-e khodi were a series of concentric circles, the smallest and most meaningful one being the family, which was surrounded by those from the same neighborhood, those from the same social circle, those with the same social standing, and eventually, those who shared the same political views on society (supporters of the Shah versus supporters of the left, Mujaheddin, etc.). Belonging to a specific political group but having a different socioeconomic status from one's political comrades meant that one's khodi circles changed based on circumstances. People in a group could identify or be identified as khodi in one instance and gheyr-e khodi in another. See also Elling, 2013, *Minorities in Iran: Nationalism and Ethnicity after Khomeini*.

8. For more on the development of the professional classes in Iran, see Vejdani, 2014, *Making History in Iran: Education, Nationalism, and Print Culture.*

9. One prime example is the filmmaker Mohsen Makhmalbaf, who was a "child of the revolution" in the sense that he received training by the government and was a supporter of the Islamic Republic in the first decade of the revolution. He received favorable treatment throughout the 1980s and 1990s, until he began to make more critical films. Today, he is exiled, and many pro-regime filmmakers talk of him with a great deal of anger and resentment. They see him as a traitor to their values and as the ultimate *gheyr-e khodi.*

10. Facial hair for men, except for a mustache, indicated religiosity. Historically, it has been considered proper in Islam for men to have beards, based on hadiths of the Prophet Mohammad. Yet, it is not one of the pillars of Islam, thus prompting debate about the need to have a beard at all and of what length.

11. For more on this, see Moazami, 2020, "The Politics of Style in Contemporary Iran."

12. It is not uncommon to see those who regularly pray or go to mosque with the back of their shoes folded in, making it easier to slip the shoes on and off.

13. For more on the role of women and veiling in postrevolutionary Iran, please see Beck and Nashat, 2004, *Women in Iran*; Esfandiari, 1997, *Reconstructed Lives: Women and Iran's Islamic Revolution*; Hoodfar, 2001, "The Veil in Their Minds and on Our Heads"; Hoodfar, 2009, "Activism under the Radar"; Moghadam, 1988, "Women, Work, and Ideology in the Islamic Republic"; Najmabadi, 1998, "Feminism in an Islamic Republic"; Najmabadi, 2005, *Women with Mustaches and Men without Beards*; Paidar, 1995, *Women and the Political Process in 20th-Century Iran*; Sedighi, 2007, *Women and Politics in Iran.*

14. A *maghna'e* is a hijab made with one piece of cloth that covers a woman's hair, neck, and shoulders. It is the accepted form of hijab for government buildings and universities. With the election of President Khatami in 1997, some pro-regime reformist women, led by parliamentarians Elahe Kulaei and Fatemeh Haghighatjoo, directly challenged the notion that the ideal female citizen should wear a black chador. Kulaei regularly appeared in Parliament wearing a colorful headscarf and light overcoat, which caused great uproar among the press and lively debates about what a pro-regime woman should look like.

15. Nail polish is forbidden for women who pray, as it is believed that the ablution cannot be properly conducted, given that the water cannot clean the nails under the polish. Recently, however, "halal" nail polish has entered the market for women who pray.

16. Abrahamian, 1989, *Radical Islam: The Iranian Mojahedin.*

17. Prior to the revolution, only 16 universities existed in Iran, enrolling about 150,000 students, with another 100,000 studying abroad. University students and

those who had traveled abroad were most likely to be labeled as *rowshanfekr*. Today, Iran has 54 state universities, 42 state medical schools, 289 major private universities, and 485 local study centers in the Payam-e Noor University system, which offers degrees remotely or online. The number of university students in Iran is now over four million, and with subsidized pilgrimage travel to Mecca, Damascus (before the civil war), Karbala, and Najaf, a large number of Iranians have traveled abroad at least once. Moreover, with travel becoming more affordable prior to increased Western sanctions surrounding the nuclear issue (2012), segments of the population that had not traditionally traveled outside Iran except for pilgrimages began to go to Turkey, Dubai, Thailand, Malaysia, and Armenia for leisure. In the hierarchy of travel destinations, those who have ventured to Europe and North America hold more distinction than those who have not. However, the range of people considered rowshanfekr has widened as university degrees and opportunities to travel have increased. For more on rowshanfekrs during the revolutionary period, see Abrahamian, 1980, "Structural Causes of the Iranian Revolution."

18. *Rowshanfekr* is not to be confused with *rowshanfekr-e mazhabi* (religious intellectuals), another term that my interlocutors didn't use define themselves. For more on religious intellectuals in the Islamic Republic, please see Boroujerdi, 1996, *Iranian Intellectuals and the West*; Dabashi, 1993, *Theology of Discontent*; Ghamari-Tabrizi, 2008, *Islam and Dissent*; Kamrava, 2008, *Iran's Intellectual Revolution*; Manoukian, 2011, *City of Knowledge in 20th-Century Iran*; Matsunaga, 2009, "Secularization of a *Faqih*-Headed Revolutionary Islamic State of Iran"; Mirsepassi, 2000, *Intellectual Discourses and the Politics of Modernization*; Mirsepassi, 2011, *Democracy in Modern Iran*; Nabavi, 2003, *Intellectuals and the State in Iran*.

19. Owing to its roots to prerevolutionary Iran, a key characteristic of the idea of rowshanfekr is a sense of alienation from traditional classes, meaning an identification with modernist notions of dress, gender roles, and comportment. Rowshanfekrs are usually thought to be and act more westernized.

20. After the international community had isolated Iran following its revolution and the American hostage crisis in 1980, Iranian cinema in the 1990s brought international recognition to the country. The "new wave of Iranian cinema," as it was called, took the world by storm with the films of Abbas Kiarostami, Mohsen Makhmalbaf, Jafar Panahi, and Majid Majidi. After a decade of isolation, these filmmakers brought recognition to their country on the most prestigious stages of cinema via the world film festival circuit: from Cannes to Berlin to Toronto, and later to Hollywood, with Asghar Farhadi's Oscar win for *A Separation* in 2012 and again in 2015 for *Salesman*. Pro-regime cultural producers lamented that the gheyr-e khodis received accolades, while the films that depicted the regime's point of view were never recognized (Azadeh Mousavi and Kouroush Ataei portray this divide in their documentary *The Making of* A Separation, 2012).

21. For more on the film's banning, see "Why Was *Desirable Garbage* Banned Forever?," *Tabnak News*, accessed April 30, 2017, *www.tabnak.ir/fa/news/424945/*.

22. For more on subcultures, please see Hebdige, (1979) 2012, *Subculture: The Making of Style.*

23. Despite the fact that the Art University of Iran is based in Tehran, like many prestigious state universities in Iran, many of the students (in some places the majority) come from the provinces.

Chapter 4: New Strategies

1. Film directors such as Abbas Kiarostami and Jafar Panahi have portrayed the car as the private realm in Iran in films such as *Taste of Cherry* (1997), *Ten* (2002), and *Taxi* (2015).

2. For more on Stuxnet, please see Sanger, 2013, *Confront and Conceal*; Zetter, 2014, *Countdown to Zero Day.*

3. Although some women choose to keep some form of hijab when they leave Iran for short trips, very rarely do they wear the official maghna'e. The only times that I have seen women outside of Iran wearing the maghna'e is when they are on an official trip organized in some way by the government.

4. The film has screened internationally as an "insider's" look into the MEK, via organizations such as Docunight, which screens documentaries about Iran on a monthly basis throughout North America.

5. Immediately after the 2009 Green Movement uprisings, Payeshenas made his first MEK film, *Molāghat Poshteh Divār-hā-ye Ashraf* (Visitation behind the Walls of Camp Ashraf, 2009). "This is the first film on Iranian television that I know of that attempted to depict the MEK more fairly," Payeshenas told me on Christmas morning at his office in 2013. The film is an introduction to the MEK, and, at Payeshenas's insistence, it refers to them as the Mujaheddin rather than the *monāfeqin* ("hypocrites"), similar to his later film, *An Unfinished Film for My Daughter Somayeh*, in order to differentiate it from other state productions. *Visitation* offers an overview of the organization and interviews with former members who now reside in Europe, Canada, and Iran, as well as Antoine Gessler, a European expert on the MEK; it also provides footage of reports on human rights abuses by the likes of the RAND Corporation. This film attempts to offer criticism of the MEK from groups and people outside the Islamic Republic to demonstrate to the viewer that many others besides the Islamic Republic are against the MEK.

6. *Memories for All Seasons* (2014) is a documentary film about chemical warfare survivors who were taken to Austria for treatment, directed by Mostafa Razaq Karimi.

7. For more on the role of music and the various constraints implemented against it in postrevolutionary Iran, see Siamdoust, 2017, *Soundtrack of the Revolution.*

8. If the film is screened on state television, audience members assume that pro-regime filmmakers made the film, a strategy that some filmmakers try to avoid in order to increase their audience size.

9. Creative ways to circulate media are not new or limited to Iran. For a rich discussion of different avenues for circulation, see Himpele, 2007, *Circuits of Culture*.

10. For more on nationalism and media, see Anderson, 2006, *Imagined Communities*; Ang, 1991, *Desperately Seeking the Audience*; Ang, 1996, *Living Room Wars*.

11. Ang, 1991, *Desperately Seeking the Audience*.

12. Williams, 2016, *Resources of Hope: Culture, Democracy, Socialism*, 196.

13. Ang, 1991, *Desperately Seeking the Audience*, 2.

14. For an in-depth look into the Bollywood film industry, see Ganti, 2012, *Producing Bollywood*.

15. For more on conceptions of the future as cultural fact, see Appadurai, 2013, *The Future as Cultural Fact*.

16. Dornfield, 1998, *Producing Public Television*, 87.

17. Dornfield, 1998.

18. *Javanmard* is a set of masculine ethical characteristics associated with being magnanimous, brave, and loyal. Javanmard and its associations with *fotowwa*, in Arabic (*fata*, "young," pl. *fetyan*), date back to initiation rituals and codes in the Islamic world, primarily in the eastern regions of Persia and what became Iraq. Imam 'Ali ibn Abi Talebi (the grandson of the Prophet Mohammad and the first Shi'a Imam) was designated as *sayyed al-fetyan*, and there is a well-known account of him as "la fata ella 'Ali'" (there is no young brave man but "Ali") during the battle of Ohod.

During the early Islamic Omayyad and 'Abbasid periods, fotowwa/javanmard took on an organizational role as urban militias of young men spread throughout Persian cities from the seventh century onwards. These militias were also instrumental in frontier regions of Persia and eventually became full-time fighters with an income. Manifestos of fotowwa, known as *fotowwa-nameh*, became linked to the *zur-khaneh*, traditional Persian gymnasiums in which these characteristics of masculinity were further tied to Imam 'Ali; a large portrait of him hangs in every zur-khaneh. See further Bahar, 1976, *Barresy-e Farhang-i Ejtema-e Zurkhaneh-ha-ye Tehran*; Yarshater, 1985–2007, *The History of al-Ṭabari*; Taeschner, 1965, "Futuwwa"; Zakeri, "From Iran to Islam: 'Ayyārān and Futuwwa"; for contemporary usage, see Adelkhah, 1999, *Being Modern in Iran*, 30–52.

Chapter 5: Producing Nationalism

Portions of this chapter are adapted with permission from Narges Bajoghli, "The IRGC's Plans to Win Hearts and Minds," *Al Monitor*, March 13, 2016.

1. In fact, as ethnographic research reveals, there is a vibrant atmosphere of people partaking in forms of religious practice. For more, see Doostdar, 2018, *The Iranian Metaphysical*.

2. I first wrote about this music video in The Guardian, "How Iran is Trying to Win Back the Youth," July 20, 2015.

3. Songwriter: Mohsen Razavaei; composer: Omid Roushanbeen; singer: Hossein Haghighi.

4. For an example of discussions of the music video on national television, see Aparat, www.aparat.com/v/Cer8R.

5. Kaveh the Blacksmith leads an uprising against a foreign invader in order to reinstate Persian rule. Rostam is the most celebrated of the heroes in the *Shāhnāmeh*, and Raksh is his famous divine horse.

6. With the U.S. ship under the command of William C. Rogers, the incident took place in Iranian airspace, over Iran's territorial waters in the Persian Gulf, and on the flight's usual path. It is still the deadliest aviation disaster in the Persian Gulf region and the eighth deadliest in the world. Two years after this incident, Rogers was awarded the Legion of Merit by the U.S. military, and no mention was made of Iran Air flight 655 or the 290 dead civilians. The United States never apologized for the incident but did reach a settlement with Iran in the International Court of Justice in 1996. The story of Iran Air flight 655 continues to loom large not only in the minds of average Iranian citizens but also, and especially, in the grand narrative of the Islamic Republic repeated by its supporters, in which the United States has again and again inflicted atrocities on Iran without apology or consequence. For more information, see UPI Archives, December 8, 1988, "U.N. Agency Issues Report on Downing of Iran Air Jet," www.upi.com/Archives/1988/12/08/UN-agency-issues-report-on-downing-of-Iran-Air-jet/6458597560400/; Max Fisher, October 16, 2013, "The Forgotten Story of Iran Air Flight 655," *Washington Post*, www.washingtonpost.com/news/worldviews/wp/2013/10/16/the-forgotten-story-of-iran-air-flight-655.

7. Filkins, 2013, "The Shadow Commander."

8. To view the documentary, see *Soleimani Documentary* (with English subtitles), Ahwaz Channel, www.aparat.com/v/qMOL0; for the music video, see www.aparat.com/v/oRkxC/.

9. Monavar Khalaj, December 1, 2015, "Security Tightened in Iran amid Fears of ISIS Attack," *Financial Times*, www.ft.com/content/8f69000a-9779-11e5-95c7-d47aa298f769.

Conclusion

Portions of this chapter are adapted with permission from Narges Bajoghli, "IRGC Media Producers Open New Front against Rouhani," *Al Monitor*, January 3, 2018.

1. To see the video, www.aparat.com/avanttv.

2. For an example of earlier discussions on anxieties over media, please see Williams, 1974, *Television: Technology and Cultural Form*.

Bibliography

Abrahamian, Ervand. 1980. "Structural Causes of the Iranian Revolution." *MERIP Reports* 87: 21–26.

———. 1989. *Radical Islam: The Iranian Mojahedin*. London: I. B. Tauris.

———. 1993. *Khomeinism: Essays on the Islamic Republic*. Berkeley: University of California Press.

———. 1999. *Tortured Confessions: Prisons and Public Recantations in Modern Iran*. Berkeley: University of California Press.

———. 2009. *A History of Modern Iran*. New York: Cambridge University Press.

———. 2009. "Why the Islamic Republic Has Survived." *Middle East Report* 250 (Spring): 10–16.

———. 2013. *The Coup: 1953, the CIA, and the Roots of Modern US-Iranian Relations*. New York: New Press.

Abu-Lughod, Lila. 1993. "Finding a Place for Islam: Egyptian Television Serials and the National Interest." *Public Culture* 5: 493–513.

———. 1997. "The Interpretation of Culture(s) after Television." *Representations* 59: 25–50.

———. 2005. *Dramas of Nationhood: The Politics of Television in Egypt*. Chicago: University of Chicago Press.

Adelkhah, Fariba. 1999. *Being Modern in Iran*. London: Hurst.

Afary, Janet. 2009. *Sexual Politics in Modern Iran*. Cambridge University Press.

Akbari, A. 1973. *Lompanism*. Tehran: Nashr-e Sepehr.

Akhavan, Niki. 2013. *Electronic Iran: The Cultural Politics of an Online Evolution*. New Brunswick, NJ: Rutgers University Press.

Alahmad, Nida, and Arang Keshavarzian. 2010. "A War on Multiple Fronts." *MERIP* (Winter).

Alavi, Nasrin. 2006. *We Are Iran*. London: Portobello Books.

Alfoneh, Ali. 2013. *Iran Unveiled: How the Revolutionary Guard Is Turning Theocracy into Military Dictatorship*. Washington, DC: AEI Press.

Algar, Hamid. 1981. *Islam and Revolution: Writings and Declarations of Imam Khomeini*. Berkeley, CA: Mizan Press.

Amiri, Nooshabeh. 2007. Interview with Masoud Dehnamaki. *Rooz Online*. June 24, 2007. www.roozonline.com/english/archives/2007/06/mdehnamaki_everybody_i_now_a.html

Anderson, Benedict. 2006. *Imagined Communities*. New York: Verso.

Ang, Ien. 1991. *Desperately Seeking the Audience*. London: Routledge.

———. 1996. *Living Room Wars: Rethinking Media Audiences for a Postmodern World*. London: Routledge.

Appadurai, Arjun. 1996. "Global Ethnoscapes: Notes and Queries for a Transnational Anthropology." In *Modernity at Large: Cultural Dimensions of Globalization*, 48–65. Minneapolis: University of Minnesota Press.

———. 2013. *The Future as Cultural Fact: Essays on the Global Condition*. New York: Verso.

Arjomand, Said Amir. 2009. *After Khomeini: Iran under His Successors*. New York: Oxford University Press.

Armbrust, Walter, ed. 2000. *Mass Mediations: New Approaches to Popular Culture in the Middle East and Beyond*. Los Angeles: University of California Press.

———. 2002. "Islamists in Egyptian Cinema." *American Anthropologist* 104 (3): 922–31.

Atabaki, Touraj, ed. 2009. *Iran in the 20th Century: Historiographic and Political Culture*. London: I. B. Tauris.

Avini, Morteza. 1991. *Ayiney-e Jadu*. Tehran: Barg Publications.

———. 1996. "Az Hadis-e Shaydaei: Koft-o-gu ba Seyed Morteza Avini, Kargardan va Nevisandeye Majmueye Mostanade Revayate Fath." *Farabi Quarterly Magazine* 7 (1:25): 1375.

Bahar, M. 1976. *Barresy-e Farhang-i Ejtema-e Zurkhaneh-ha-ye Tehran*. Tehran: High Council of Culture and Art.

Bajoghli, Narges. 2014. "Digital Media as Surveillance." In *Wired Citizenship: Youth Learning and Activisim in the Middle East*, edited by Linda Herrera and Rehab Sakr, 180–194. New York: Routledge.

———. 2017. "*The Outcasts*: The Start of 'New Entertainment' in Pro-Regime Filmmaking in the Islamic Republic of Iran." *Middle East Critique* 26(1).

———. Forthcoming. "The Researcher as National Security Threat: Surveillance, Agency, and Entanglement in Iran and the United States." *Journal of Contemporary Studies of South Asia, Africa, and the Middle East*.

Bakhash, Shaul. 1990. *Iran under the Ayatollahs*. New York: Basic Books.

Balaghi, Shiva. 2003. *Picturing Iran*. London: I. B. Tauris.

Basmenji, Kaveh. 2005. *Tehran Blues: Youth Culture in Iran*. London: Saqi Books.

Bayat, Asef. 1997. *Street Politics: Poor People's Movement in Iran*. New York: Columbia University Press.

———. 2013. *Life as Politics: How Ordinary People Change the Middle East*. Stanford, CA: Stanford University Press.

Beck, Lois, and Guity Nashat, eds. 2004. *Women in Iran: From 1800 to the Islamic Republic*. Champaign: University of Illinois Press.

Behrooz, Maziar. 1999. *Rebels with a Cause: The Failure of the Left in Iran*. New York: I. B. Tauris.

Behrouzan, Orkideh. 2016. *Prozak Diaries: Psychiatry and Generational Memory in Iran*. Stanford, CA: Stanford University Press.

Bishara, Amahl, 2012. *Back Stories: US News Production and Palestinian Politics*. Stanford, CA: Stanford University Press.

Bloch, Maurice, ed. 1975. *Political Language and Oratory in Traditional Society*. London: Academic Press.

Boroujerdi, Mehrzad. 1996. *Iranian Intellectuals and the West: The Tormented Triumph of Nativism*. Syracuse, NY: Syracuse University Press.

Bourdieu, Pierre. 1979. "Symbolic Power." *Critique of Anthropology* 4, no. 13–14: 77–85.

———. 1993. *The Field of Cultural Production*. New York: Columbia University Press

———. 1998. *On Television*. New York: New Press.

Boyer, Dominic. 2003. "Censorship as a vocation: The institutions, practices, and cultural logic of media control in the German Democratic Republic." In *Comparative Studies in Society and History*, 45(3), 511–545.

———. 2007. *Understanding Media: A Popular Philosophy*. Chicago: Prickly Paradigm Press.

Buchta, Wilfried. 2002. *Who Rules Iran*. Washington, DC: Washington Institute for Near East Policy.

Buck-Morss, Susan. 2002. *Dreamworld and Catastrophe: The Passing of Mass Utopia in East and West*. Cambridge, MA: MIT Press.

Caldwell, John. 2008. *Production Culture*. Durham, NC: Duke University Press.

Chaqueri, Cosroe. 2001. *Origins of Social Democracy in Modern Iran*. Seattle: University of Washington Press.

Chehabi, Houchang. 1990. *Iranian Politics and Religious Modernism*. Ithaca, NY: Cornell University Press.

Chelkowski, Peter, and Hamid Dabashi. 1999. *Staging a Revolution: The Art of Persuasion in the Islamic Republic of Iran*. New York: New York University Press.

Chubin, Shahram, and Charles Tripp. 1988. *Iran and Iraq at War*. Boulder, CO: Westview Press.

Cronin, Stephanie. 2004. *Reformers and Revolutionaries in Modern Iran*. London: Routledge.

———. 2010. *Soldiers, Shahs and Subalterns in Iran: Opposition, Protest and Revolt (1921–41)*. London: Palgrave.

Corney, Frederick C. 1998. "Rethinking a Great Event: The October Revolution as Memory Project." *Social Science History* 22, no. 04: 389–414.

———. 2004. *Telling October: Memory and the Making of the Bolshevik Revolution*. Ithaca, NY: Cornell University Press.

Dabashi, Hamid. 1993. *Theology of Discontent*. New York: New York University Press.

———. 2001. *Close Up: Iranian Cinema, Past, Present and Future*. London; New York: Verso.

———. 2007a. *Iran: A People Interrupted*. New York: New Press.

———. 2007b. *Masters and Masterpieces of Iranian Cinema*. Washington, DC: Mage Publishers.

Danesh, Mehrzad. 2007. "Khashm va khandeh va faryad." *Film* (Farvardin 1386): 33–34.

De Bellaigue, Christopher. 2006. *In the Rose Garden of the Martyrs*. New York: Harper Perennial.

Deeb, Lara and Jessica Winegar. 2015. *Anthropology's Politics: Disciplining the Middle East*. Stanford, CA: Stanford University Press.

Deer, Patrick. 2009. *Culture in Camouflage: War, Empire, and Modern British Literature*. Oxford, UK: Oxford University Press.

Dehnamaki, Masoud. Blog, http://www.ekhrajiiha.blogfa.com/.

Devictor, Agnes. 2002. "Classic Tools, Original Goals: Cinema and Public Policy in the Islamic Republic of Iran." In *The New Iranian Cinema*, edited by Richard Tapper. London: I. B. Taurus.

Doostdar, Alireza. 2018. *The Iranian Metaphysicals: Explorations in Science, Islam, and the Uncanny*. Princeton, NJ: Princeton University Press.

Dornfield, Barry. 1998. *Producing Public Television*. Princeton, NJ: Princeton University Press.

Dowell, Kristin L. 2013. *Sovereign Screens: Aboriginal Media on the Canadian West Coast*. Lincoln: University of Nebraska Press.

Elling, Rasmus Christian. 2013. *Minorities in Iran: Nationalism and Ethnicity after Khomeini*. New York: Palgrave Macmillan.

Ellul, Jacques. 1973. *Propaganda: The Formation of Men's Attitudes*. New York: Vintage.

Erami, Narges. 2008. "Rates of Influence: Revolution, Religion, and Ritual in a Holy
    Iranian City." PhD diss., Columbia University.

Esfandiari, Haleh. 1997. *Reconstructed Lives: Women and Iran's Islamic Revolution*. Wash-
    ington, DC: Woodrow Wilson Center Press with Johns Hopkins University Press.

Farhi, Farideh. 1990. *State and Urban-Based Revolution: Iran and Nicaragua*. Cham-
    paign: University of Illinois Press.

———. 2006. "The Antimonies of Iran's War Generation." In *Iran, Iraq, and the Legacies
    of War*, edited by Lawrence Potter and Gary Sick. New York: Palgrave Macmillan.

Fathi, Nazila. 2005. "A Revolutionary Channels His Inner Michael Moore." *New York
    Times*. November 26, 2005. www.nytimes.com/2005/11/26/world/middleeast/a
    -revolutionary-channels-his-inner-michael-moore.html.

Filkins, Dexter. 2013. "The Shadow Commander." *New Yorker*, September 30, 2013.
    www.newyorker.com/magazine/2013/09/30/the-shadow-commander.Fischer,
    Michael. 2003. *Iran: From Religious Dispute to Revolution*. Madison: University
    of Wisconsin Press.

———. 2004. *Mute Dreams, Blind Owls, and Dispersed Knowledge*. Durham, NC:
    Duke University Press.

Fitzpatrick, Sheila, Alexander Rabinowitch, and Richard Stites, eds. 1991. *Russia in
    the Era of NEP: Explorations in Soviet Society and Culture*. Bloomington: Indiana
    University Press.

Floor, Willem M. 1981. "The Political Role of the Lutis in Iran." In *Modern Iran: The
    Dialectics of Continuity and Change*, edited by Michael E. Bonine and Nikki Ked-
    die. Albany: State University of New York Press.

Foucault, Michel. 1986 "Of Other Spaces." *Diacritics* 16, no. 1: 22–27.

Ganti, Tejaswini. 2012. *Producing Bollywood: Inside the Contemporary Hindi Film
    Industry*. Durham, NC: Duke University Press.

Gellner, Ernest. 2009. *Nations and Nationalism*. Ithaca, NY: Cornell University Press.

Ghamari-Tabrizi, Behrooz. 2008. *Islam and Dissent*. London: I. B. Tauris.

Gilsenan, Michael. 1996. *Lords of the Lebanese Marches: Violence and Narrative in an
    Arab Society*. Berkeley: University of California Press.

Ginsburg, Faye. 1994. "Culture/Media: A (Mild) Polemic." *Anthropology Today* 10,
    no. 2: 5–15.

Ginsburg, Faye, Lila Abu-Lughod, and Brian Larkin. 2002. *Media Worlds: Anthropol-
    ogy on New Terrain*. Berkeley: University of California Press.

Golkar, Saeid. 2010a. "The Ideological-Political Training of Iran's Basij." *Middle East
    Brief* 44 (September 2010). www.brandeis.edu/crown/publications/meb/meb44
    .html.

———. 2010b. "The Reign of Hard-line Students in Iran's Universities." *Middle East
    Quarterly* (Summer 2010).

———. 2011. "Politics of Piety: The Basij and Moral Control of Iranian Society." *Journal of the Middle East and Africa* 2, no. 2: 207–19.

———. 2012. "Paramilitarization of the Economy: The Case of Iran's Basij Militia." *Armed Forces and Society* 38, no.4: 625–48.

———. 2015. *Captive Society: The Basij Militia and Social Control in Iran*. Washington, DC: Woodrow Wilson Center Press.

Gordon, Joel. 2000. "*Nasser 56*/Cairo 96: Reimagining Egypt's Lost Community." In *Mass Mediations: New Approaches to Popular Culture of the Middle East and Beyond*, edited by Walter Armbrust, 161–81. Berkeley: University of California Press.

Grant, Bruce. 2014. "The Edifice Complex: Architecture and the Political Life of Surplus in the New Baku." *Public Culture* 26, no. 3: 501–28.

Gupta, Akhil. 1995. "Blurred Boundaries: The Discourse of Corruption, the Culture of Politics, and the Imagined State." *American Ethnologist* 22, no. 2: 375–402.

Gupta, Akhil, and James Ferguson. 1992. "Beyond 'Culture': Space, Identity and the Politics of Difference." *Cultural Anthropology* 7, no. 1: 6–23.

———. 1997. *Culture, Power, Place: Explorations in Critical Anthropology*. Durham, NC: Duke University Press.

Haeri, Shahla. 2014. *Law of Desire: Temporary Marriage in Shi'i Iran*. Syracuse, NY: Syracuse University Press.

Harris, Kevan. 2012. "The Brokered Exuberance of the Middle Class: An Ethnographic Analysis of Iran's 2009 Green Movement." *Mobilization* 17, no. 6: 435–55.

———. 2013. "The Rise of the Subcontractor State: Politics of Pseudo-Privatization in the Islamic Republic of Iran." *International Journal of Middle East Studies* 45, no. 1: 45–70.

———. 2016. "All the Sepah's Men: Iran's Revolutionary Guards in Theory and Practice." In *Businessmen in Arms: How the Military and Other Armed Groups Profit in the MENA Region*, edited by Elke Grawert and Zeinab Abul-Magd, 97–118. Lanham, MD: Rowman & Littlefield.

———. 2017. *A Social Revolution: Politics and the Welfare State in Iran*. Oakland: University of California Press.

Hebdige, Dick. (1979) 2012. *Subculture: The Making of Style*. London: Routledge.

Himpele, Jeff. 2007. *Circuits of Culture: Media, Politics, and Indigenous Identity in the Andes*. Minneapolis: University of Minnesota Press.

Hiro, Dilip. 1985. *Iran under the Ayatollahs*. London: Routledge and Kegan Paul.

Hirschkind, Charles. 2009. *The Ethical Landscape*. New York: Columbia University Press.

Hoodfar, Homa. 2001. "The Veil in Their Minds and on Our Heads: Veiling Practices and Muslim Women." In *Women, Gender, Religion: A Reader*, edited by Elizabeth Castelli, 420–46. New York: Palgrave Macmillan.

———. 2009. "Activism under the Radar: Volunteer Women Health Workers in Iran." *Middle East Report* 250 (Spring): 56–60.

Hooglund, Eric. 2009. "Thirty Years of Islamic Revolution in Rural Iran." *Middle East Report* 250 (Spring): 34–39.

Irvine, Judith T. 1979. "Formality and Informality in Communicative Events." *American Anthropologist* 81, no. 4: 773–90.

Jackson, John. 2005. *Real Black: Adventures in Racial Sincerity*. Chicago: University of Chicago Press.

Kamalipour, Yahya, ed. 2010. *Media, Power, and Politics in the Digital Age: The 2009 Presidential Election Uprising in Iran*. Lanham, MD: Rowman & Littlefield.

Kamrava, Mehran. 2008. *Iran's Intellectual Revolution*. Cambridge, UK: Cambridge University Press.

Karimi, I. 1990. "Qahreman ya Qorbani." *Mahnameh-ye Sinemai-ye Film* (Dey 1369): 52–54.

Kashani-Sabet, Firoozeh. 2000. *Frontier Fictions: Shaping the Iranian Nation, 1804–1946*. Princeton, NJ: Princeton University Press.

Kazemi, Farhad. 1980. *Poverty and Revolution in Iran: The Migrant Poor, Urban Marginality, and Politics*. New York: New York University Press.

Keddie, Nikki. 2003. *Modern Iran: Roots and Results of Revolution*. New Haven, CT: Yale University Press.

Keshavarzian, Arang. 2003. "Turban or Hat, Seminarian or Soldier: State Building and Clergy Building in Reza Shah's Iran." *Journal of Church and State* 45, no. 1: 81–112.

———. 2005. "Contestation Without Democracy: Elite Fragmentation in Iran." In *Authoritarianism in the Middle East: Regimes and Resistance*, edited by Marsha Pripstein Posusney and Michele Penner Angrist, 63–89. Boulder, CO: Lynne Riemer.

———. 2009. *Bazaar and State in Iran: The Politics of the Tehran Marketplace*. Cambridge, UK: Cambridge University Press.

Keshavarzian, Arang, and Narges Erami. 2015. "When Ties Don't Bind: Smuggling Effects, Bazaars, and Regulatory Regimes in Post-revolutionary Iran. *Economy and Society* 44, no. 1.

Khamenei, Seyyed Ali. 1994. *Farhang va Tahajom-e Farhangi*. Tehran: Sazman-e Farhangi-ye Enqelab-e Eslami.

Khomeini, Ruhollah. 1981. *Velayat-e Faqih: Hokumat-e Eslami*. Tehran: Amir Kabir.

———. 1989. "Last Will and Testament." Al-Islam.org. https://www.al-islam.org/printpdf/book/export/html/39086.

Khooshkhoo, Arash. 2007. "Chera *Ekhrajiha* Filme Khubi Nist." *40Cheragh* (Farvardin 1386).

Khosravi, Shahram. 2008. *Young and Defiant in Tehran*. Philadelphia: University of Pennsylvania Press.

Khoury, Dina Rizk. 2013. *Iraq in Wartime: Soldiering, Martyrdom, and Remembrance*. Cambridge, UK: Cambridge University Press.

Kian-Thiébaut, Azadeh. 2002. "Women and the Making of Civil Society in the Post-Islamist Iran." In *Twenty Years of Islamic Revolution*, edited by Eric Hooglund. Syracuse, NY: Syracuse University Press.

Kurzman, Charles. 2004. *The Unthinkable Revolution in Iran*. Cambridge, MA: Harvard University Press.

Larkin, Brian. 2008. *Signal and Noise*. Durham, NC: Duke University Press.

Lasswell, Harold. 1927. *Propaganda Technique in the World War*. New York: Knopf.

Mahdavi, Pardis. 2008. *Passionate Uprisings: Iran's Sexual Revolution*. Stanford, CA: Stanford University Press.

Malekzadeh, Shervin. 2011. "Schooled to Obey, Learning to Protest: The Ambiguous Outcomes of Postrevolutionary Schooling in the Islamic Republic of Iran." PhD thesis, Georgetown University. ProQuest Dissertations (PQDT 3450846).

Mankekar, Purnima. 1999. *Screening Culture, Viewing Politics: An Ethnography of Television, Womanhood, and Nation in Post-colonial India*. Durham, NC: Duke University Press.

Mannheim, Karl. 1970. "The Problem of Generations." *Psychoanalytic Review* 57, no. 3.

Manoukian, Setrag. 2011. *City of Knowledge in Twentieth-Century Iran: Shiraz, History, and Poetry*. Oxford, UK; New York: Routledge.

Matsunaga, Yasuyuki. 2009. "Secularization of a *Faqih*-Headed Revolutionary Islamic State of Iran: Its Mechanisms, Processes, and Prospects." *Comparative Studies of South Asia, Africa and the Middle East* 29, 3: 468–82.

Mayer, Vicki. 2011. *Below the Line*. Durham, NC: Duke University Press.

Mayer, Vicki, Miranda Banks, and John Caldwell, eds. 2009. *Production Studies*. Oxford, UK; New York: Routledge.

Mazzarella, William. 2004. "Culture, Globalization, Mediation." *Annual Review of Anthropology* 33: 345–67.

———. 2013. *Censorium*. Durham, NC: Duke University Press.

McLuhan, Marshall. 1964. *Understanding Media: The Extensions of Man*. London: Routledge and Kegan Paul.

Mehrabi, M. 1984. *Tarikh-e Sinema-ye Iran az Aghaz ta Sal-e 1357*. Tehran: Entesharat-e Film.

Mir-Hosseini, Ziba. 1999. *Islam and gender: The religious debate in contemporary Iran*. Princeton, NJ: Princeton University Press.

———. 2000. *Marriage on Trial: A Study of Islamic Family Law*. London: I. B. Tauris.

Mirsepassi, Ali. 2000. *Intellectual Discourse and the Politics of Modernization: Negotiating Modernity in Iran*. Cambridge, UK: Cambridge University Press, 2000.

———. 2011. *Democracy in Modern Iran*. New York: New York University Press.

Moaddel, Mansoor. 1992. *Class, Politics, and Ideology in the Iranian Revolution*. New York: Columbia University Press.

Moazami, Morad. 2020. "The Politics of Style in Contemporary Iran: Mod, Media, and Modernization from 1965–1985." PhD thesis, Oxford University.

Moazezinia, Hossein. 2007. "Film-e jangi-e irani va tamashagarash: Aya sinema-ye def'a moghadas mokhatebash ra peyda kardeh ast?" *Dunya-e Tasvir* (Mordad 1386): 49–51.

Moghadam, Val. 1988. "Women, Work, and Ideology in the Islamic Republic." *International Journal of Middle Eastern Studies* 20: 221–43.

Moghissi, Haideh. 2016. *Populism and Feminism in Iran: Women's Struggle in a Male-Defined Revolutionary Movement*. New York: Springer.

Montagne, Renee. 2008. "The Evolution of Iran's Revolutionary Guard." *Morning Edition*, National Public Radio, April 5, 2007. www.npr.org/templates/story/story.php?storyId=9371072.

Moosavi, Amir. 2015. "Dust That Never Settled: Ideology, Ambivalence and Disenchantment in Arabic and Persian Fiction of the Iran-Iraq war (1980–2003)." PhD thesis, New York University.

Moruzzi, Norma Claire and Fatemeh Sadeghi. 2006. "Out of the Frying Pan, into the Flame: Young Iranian Women Today," *Middle East Report* 241 (Winter): 22–28.

Moslem, Mehdi. 2002. *Factional Politics in Post-Khomeini Iran*. Syracuse, NY: Syracuse University Press.

Mottahedeh, Negar. 2007. *Representing the Unrepresentable: Historical Images of National Reform from the Qajars to the Islamic Republic of Iran*. Syracuse, NY: Syracuse University Press.

———. 2008. *Displaced Allegories: Post-Revolutionary Iranian Cinema*. Durham, NC: Duke University Press.

———. 2015. *#iranelection: Hashtag Solidarity and the Transformation of Online Life*. Stanford, CA: Stanford University Press.

Mottahedeh, Roy. 1985. *The Mantle of the Prophet: Religion and Politics in Iran*. New York: Simon and Schuster.

Nabavi, Negin. 2003. *Intellectuals and the State in Iran: Politics, Discourse, and the Dilemma of Authenticity*. Gainesville: University Press of Florida.

Naficy, Hamid. 2001a. *An Accented Cinema: Exilic and Diasporic Filmmaking*. Princeton, NJ: Princeton University Press.

———. 2001b. "Iranian Cinema." In *Companion Encyclopedia of Middle Eastern and North African Film*, edited by Oliver Leaman. London: Routledge.

———. 2002. "Islamizing Film Culture in Iran: A Post-Khatami Update." In *The New Iranian Cinema*, edited by Richard Tapper. London: I. B. Taurus.

———. 2011–12. *A Social History of Iranian Cinema*. 4 vols. Durham, NC: Duke University Press.

Najmabadi, Afsaneh. 1998. "Feminism in an Islamic Republic." In *Islam, Gender, and Social Change*, edited by Yvonne Haddad and John Esposito, 59–84. New York: Oxford University Press.

———. 2005. *Women with Mustaches and Men without Beards: Gender and Sexual Anxieties of Iranian Modernity.* Berkeley: University of California Press.

———. 2013. *Professing Selves: Transsexuality and Same-Sex Desire in Contemporary Iran.* Durham, NC: Duke University Press.

Nasrabadi, Manijeh. Forthcoming. *Neither Washington, Nor Tehran: Iranian Revolutionaries in the United States.* Durham, NC: Duke University Press.

Ohem, Steven. 2012. *Iran's Revolutionary Guard: The Threat That Grows While America Sleeps.* Dulles, VA: Potomac Books.

Osanloo, Arzoo. 2009. *The Politics of Women's Rights in Iran.* Princeton, NJ: Princeton University Press.

Ostovar, Afshon. 2016. *Vanguard of the Imam: Religion, Politics, and Iran's Revolutionary Guard.* New York: Oxford University Press.

Ottolenghi, Emanuele. 2011. *The Pasdaran: Inside Iran's Islamic Revolutionary Guard Corps.* Washington, DC: Foundation for Defense of Democracies Press.

Paidar, Parvin. 1995. *Women and the Political Process in 20th-Century Iran.* Cambridge, UK: Cambridge University Press.

Parsa, Misagh. 1989. *Social Origins of the Iranian Revolution.* New Brunswick, NJ: Rutgers University Press.

Rajagopal, Arvind. 2001. *Politics after Television: Hindu Nationalism and the Reshaping of the Public in India.* Cambridge, UK: Cambridge University Press.

Rastegar, Kamran. 2015. *Surviving Images: Cinema, War, and Cultural Memory in the Middle East.* New York: Oxford University Press.

Sabet, Farzan, and Roozbeh Safshekan. 2013. *Soft War: A New Episode in the Old Conflict between Iran and the United States.* Philadelphia: Iran Media Program, Center for Global Communication Studies, Annenberg School for Communication, University of Pennsylvania. https://global.asc.upenn.edu/app/uploads/2014/06/soft_war_0.pdf.

Sadr, Hamid. 2006. *Iranian Cinema: A Political History.* London: I. B. Taurus.

Salamandra, Christa. 1998. "Moustache Hairs Lost: Ramadan Television Serials and the Construction of Identity in Damascus, Syria." Special issue: Visual Culture in the Middle East, *Visual Anthropology* 10, no. 2–4: 227–46.

———. 2012a. "The Muhannad Effect: Media Panic, Melodrama, and the Arab Female Gaze." *Anthropological Quarterly* 85, no. 1: 45–78.

———. 2012b. "Prelude to an Uprising: Syrian Fictional Television and Socio-Political Critique." *Jadaliyya* (ezine), May 17, 2012. www.jadaliyya.com/Details/25966/Prelude-to-an-Uprising-Syrian-Fictional-Television-and-Socio-Political-Critique.

———. 2011a. "Arab Television Drama in the Satellite Era." In *Soap Operas and Tele-novelas in the Digital Age*, edited by Diana Rios and Mari Castaneda, 275–90. New York: Peter Lang Publishing.

———. 2011b. "Spotlight on the Bashar al-Asad Era: The Television Drama Outpouring." *Middle East Critique* 20, no. 2: 157–67.

———. 2013. "Arab Television Drama Production and the Islamic Public Sphere." In *Rhetoric of the Image: Visual Culture in Muslim Contexts*, edited by Christiane Gruber and Sune Haugbølle. Bloomington: Indiana University Press.

Sanger, David E. 2013. *Confront and Conceal: Obama's Secret Wars and Surprising Use of American Power*. New York: Broadway Books.

Schayegh, Cyrus. 2009. *Who Is Knowledgeable Is Strong*. Berkeley: University of California Press.

———. 2010. "'Seeing Like a State.' An Essay on the Historiography of Modern Iran." *International Journal of Middle East Studies* 42: 37–61.

Schieffelin, Bambi. 2008. "Speaking Only Your Own Mind: Reflections on Confession, Gossip, and Intentionality in Bosavi (PNG)." *Anthropological Quarterly* 81, no. 2: 431–41.

Sedighi, Hamideh. 2007. *Women and Politics in Iran: Veiling, Unveiling, and Reveiling*. Cambridge, UK: Cambridge University Press.

Siamdoust, Nahid. 2017. *Soundtrack of the Revolution: The Politics of Music in Iran*. Stanford, CA: Stanford University Press.

Skocpol, Theda. 1982. "Rentier State and Shi'a Islam in the Iranian Revolution." *Theory and Society* 11, no. 3, 265–83.

Sreberny, Annabelle, and Gholam Khiabany. 2010. *Blogistan: The Internet and Politics in Iran*. London: I. B. Tauris.

Sreberny-Mohammadi, Annabelle, and Ali Mohammadi. 1994. *Small Media, Big Revolution*. Minneapolis: University of Minnesota Press.

Stanley, Jason. 2015. *How Propaganda Works*. Princeton, NJ: Princeton University Press.

Taeschner, Franz. 1965. "Futuwwa." In *Encyclopedia of Islam*, 2nd ed. (*EI2*). Vol. 2, C–G, 961–69. Leiden: Brill.Talebi, Shahla. 2011. *Ghosts of Revolution: Rekindled Memories of Imprisonment in Iran*. Stanford, CA: Stanford University Press.

Tapper, Richard. 2002. *The New Iranian Cinema: Politics, Representation and Identity*. London: I. B. Tauris.

Tawasil, Amina. 2013. "The Howzevi (Seminarian) Women in Iran: Constituting and Reconstituting Paths." PhD thesis, Columbia University. ProQuest Dissertations Publishing.

Taylor, Phillip M. 2003. *Munitions of the Mind: A History of Propaganda from the Ancient World to the Present Day*. 3rd ed. Manchester, UK: Manchester University Press

Varzi, Roxanne. 2002. "A Ghost in the Machine: The Cinema of the Iranian Sacred Defense." In *The New Iranian Cinema*, edited by Richard Tapper. London: I. B. Taurus.

———. 2006. *Warring Souls: Youth, Media, and Martyrdom in Post-revolution Iran*. Durham, NC: Duke University Press.

Vejdani, Farzin. 2014. *Making History in Iran: Education, Nationalism, and Print Culture*. Stanford, CA: Stanford University Press.

Wedeen, Lisa. (1999) 2015. *Ambiguities of Domination: Politics, Rhetoric, and Symbols in Contemporary Syria*. With a new preface. Chicago: University of Chicago Press.

Wellman, Rose. 2014. "Feeding Moral Relations: The Making of Kinship and Nation in Iran." PhD diss., Department of Anthropology, University of Virginia.

Williams, Raymond. 1974. *Television: Technology and Cultural Form*. London: Routledge.

———. 1977. *Marxism and Literature*. Oxford, UK: Oxford University Press.

———. 2016. *Resources of Hope: Culture, Democracy, Socialism*. London: Verso Books.

Yaghmaian, Behzad. 2002. *Social Change in Iran*. Albany: State University of New York Press.

Yarshater, Efshan, ed. 1985–2007. *The History of al-Ṭabari (Ta'riḵ al-rosol wa'l-moluk)*. By Moḥammad b. Jarir Ṭabari. Translated by various scholars. 40 vols. State University of New York Press: Albany, New York.

Yurchak, Alexei. 2013. *Everything Was Forever, Until It Was No More: The Last Soviet Generation*. Princeton, NJ: Princeton University Press.

Zakeri, Mohsen. 1995. "From Iran to Islam: 'Ayyārān and Futuwwa." In *Proceedings of the Second European Conference of Iranian Studies*, edited by Bert G. Fragner et al., 745–57. Rome: Istituto italiano per il Medio ed Estremo Oriente.

Zetter, Kim. 2014. *Countdown to Zero Day: Stuxnet and the Launch of the World's First Digital Weapon*. New York: Crown.

Zeydabadi-Nejad, Saeed. 2009. *The Politics of Iranian Cinema: Film and Society in the Islamic Republic*. Oxford, UK; New York: Routledge.

Index

Abadan, Iran, 2, 20–22, 29, 33, 47, 93–94, 131n5. *See also* oil
activism, 10, 17, 41–42, 68–69, 74–75, 113, 116. *See also* the Green Movement (2009); protests
Afshari, Nasser, 56–58
Agence Shishei (Hatamikia), 56
Ahmadinejad, Mahmoud: administration of, 27, 37, 57, 70; election of, 2, 36; presidency of, 15, 18; reelection of, 7, 26; responses to, 3, 58, 68; supporters of, 102. *See also* the Green Movement
Ahmadzadeh, Habib, 93–95
Ahvaz, Iran, 20
al-Qaeda, 19, 40, 72
American hostage crisis, 6, 137n20
Amir-Youssefi, Mohsen, 66–67, 71, 73–74, 76, 79–80
Ansār-e Hezbollah, ix, 13, 21, 27, 66
Arak, Iran, 33, 45
"Art Circle" (university organization), 9–10, 39, 119

Artesh, 30–31
Art University in Tehran, 21, 25, 39–40, 92, 138n23
Asaluyeh, Iran, 132n14
Āshgal-hā-ye Dust-dāshtani (Amir-Youssefi), 68
assassinations, 17, 68–75, 84, 90, 133n21, 135n5
audiences: biases of, 21, 98–99, 138n8; dismissal by the, 7, 91, 94, 116; loss of, 80, 114, 138n8; young, ix, 25, 94–98, 107, 116. *See also* propaganda; regime cultural producers; regime media producers; state television
AvaNet TV, 113–16
Avini, Morteza, 24, 26–28, 51, 59–60, 130n1

Baʿathist regime, 96
the Basij: centers of, 31–32; changes to, 36–37, 47; creation of, 29, 31–33, 35; divisions of, 33–34, 38;

fear of, 19, 68, 73, 81; generations of, 14, 18, 35–36, 46–48, 50, 73, 76; leaders of, 66–67, 75; power of, 8–10, 33, 35, 37; representations of, 9, 16, 19–21, 31, 45, 61, 102–3; as social network, 25, 38–39, 45–46, 55; universities and, 21, 24, 39–40, 49, 81, 119; youth of, 9, 12–13, 25, 107. *See also* the Iranian Revolution (1979); the Iran-Iraq War; protests; regime (Iranian); regime cultural producers; regime media producers; the Revolutionary Guard; soldiers; war

battlefields, 2, 20, 39, 51–52, 59. *See also* propaganda; state television; veterans; war

BBC Persian, 41, 43–44. *See also* journalism; media

Behtarin mojasame-ye Donyā (Ahmadzadeh), 93–95

The Best Statue in the World (Ahmadzadeh), 93–95

Bitter Dream (Amir-Youssefi), 66

bombs, 8, 22, 29, 63, 68, 109. *See also* fear; war

Bonyad-e Revāyat, 60, 63

Bonyād-e Shahid, 52–53

Book of Kings (Ferdowsi), 101

Britain, 44, 131n5

Bush, George W., 44

Camp Ashraf, 84, 89–90

Canada, 89–90

Cannes Film Festival, 66

censorship: of citizens, 2–3, 24; of media, 27–28, 68, 75, 79; political, 55, 60, 77; power of, 23, 70, 118. *See also* film; film festivals; government (Iran); media; propaganda

Center for the Chronicles of Victory, 26–27, 34, 50

the Central Bank, 131n14

chador, 8, 10–11, 18, 24, 78, 81, 90, 136n14. *See also* clothing; policing; women

Channel 3 (television), 55

Chronicles of Victory (Avini), 59

Cinema House, 21

Cinema Verité Film Festival (Tehran), 20, 87

City of the Sacred Defense Cinema, 60–61

classism, 7, 22–23, 29–31, 45–46, 55, 79, 116, 137n19. *See also* economics

clothing: men and, 10, 26–27, 136n10; piety and, 24, 26–27; policing of, 11, 37, 40, 61, 72, 93; politics and, 8, 10, 74, 77–78; soldiers and, 33, 73; symbolism of, 11, 14, 18, 66–67, 76–78, 81, 90, 105. *See also* masculinity; protests; social life; soldiers; women

CNN (network), 40

Cold War, 6

communication, 11–12, 89, ix. *See also* dialogue

counterrevolutionaries, 18, 30, 75, 135. *See also* the Iranian Revolution (1979)

culture: capital of, 80, 82; centers of, 16, 18, 21, 26, 55, 61, 106; control of, ix, 27, 47, 69, 72, 106; creation of, 35, 50–51, 55, 64, 77, 95; politics and, 7, 9, 35, 91; wars of, x, 10, 39, 58, 60, 99; and Western influence, 39, 70, 132n18. *See also* media; music; propaganda; regime cultural producers; social life; social media; war

Culture Committee, 94

Daesh, 4

Darya-Gholi, 93–94

Dehnamaki, Masoud, ix
Desirable Garbage (Amir-Youssefi), 68
dialogue, 12, 14, 18, 75, 80. *See also*
    communication
diaspora, 42–43, 45, 79–80, 82, 97, 104.
    See also Europe; Iran; Los Angeles,
    California; Middle East; satellite
    television
dissimulation, 7, 91–93, 117
Dornfeld, Barry, 98

economics, 113–15
An Elegy for the Loved (Soleimania),
    62–64, 83
emigration, 41, 118. *See also* diaspora;
    Los Angeles, California
entertainment, ix, 45. *See also* filmmak-
    ing; media; music; social media;
    state television
ethnography, 15, 20, 119, 122
Europe, 22, 39–46, 57, 84, 89, 93, 102,
    118, 137n17. *See also* Britain; *spe-
    cific countries*
executions, 17, 68–75, 84, 90, 133n21,
    135n5
exile, 6, 28, 41–43, 104, 114. *See also*
    diaspora; the Shah

Facebook, 45, 110. *See also* social media
factionalism, 110, 114–15
faith, 8, 16, 27, 33, 55. *See also* Islam
Fajr Film Festival, 20, 66–68, 80
families: conflict within, 71, 77, 118;
    and parenting, 47–49, 118–19;
    relationships within, 19, 25, 113,
    135n7; role of, 24, 79, 99, 118
Farabi Cinema Foundation, 58, 71,
    135n4
Farhadi, Ashgar, 54, 66, 137n20
farhang-e defā'e moghadas, 58
Farsi1, 43

Fars News Agency, 66, 70–71, 73–74,
    135n2
fear: of the Basij, 68, 78; politics and,
    17, 27, 38, 112, 121; power of, 7, 22,
    115; spies and, 19–20, 43; tactics of,
    10, 16, 47, 70; terrorism and, 20, 86;
    of Western influence, 19, 132n18.
    See also the Basij; the Iran-Iraq
    War; policing; propaganda; pro-
    tests; the Revolutionary Guard; war
fieldwork (ethnographic), 15–16, 20
*Film-e Nātamāmi Barā-ye Dokhtaram
    Somayeh* (Payeshenas), 87, 88, 89
film festivals, 20, 54, 79, 95–97
filmmaking: as career, 25, 53–55,
    87; censorship and, 5, 21, 34, 68,
    70–71, 92, 132n18; challenges of,
    ix, x, 50, 79; choices of, 51, 71; cost
    of, 28, 47, 54–55, 61, 71, 135n4; in-
    stitutions of, 21, 56, 59, 73, 132n18;
    networks and, 18, 24, 64–66, 80,
    87, 99. *See also* "Art Circle" (uni-
    versity organization); the Basij;
    censorship; culture; media; propa-
    ganda; regime cultural producers;
    the Revolutionary Guard; storytell-
    ing; universities; veterans; war;
    specific films
Foundation for the Oppressed, 132n14
funerals, 110–11, 117

Gaza, 74
GemTV, 43
generations: communication across,
    1, 5, 10–11; consistency between,
    110–11; differences between, 4, 9,
    14–15, 25–49; new, 12, 28, 35, 117.
    See also the Basij; families; protests;
    the Revolutionary Guard; soldiers;
    storytelling
Germany, 43–44, 57–58

gheyr-e khodi, 2, 54, 66, 74, 76–80, 82,
117, 135n6–135n7, 136n9
The Glass Agency (Hatamikia), 56–57
Gooya.com, 44
government (Iran), 13, 72–73, 114. *See
also* monarchism; politics; regime
(Iranian)
the Green Movement (2009): impacts
of, 4, 7, 28, 43, 72, 83, 102, 114,
138n5; and MEK, 84–86, 115; pro-
testers of, 2, 15, 66, 134n1; support
for, 12, 27, 51, 73–74; suppression
of, 3, 15, 38, 99, 106, 116; as turning
point, 1, 9, 105, 107, 111; violence
and, 34, 68, 75–76. *See also* the
Basij; culture; families; filmmaking;
government (Iran); policing; propaganda; protests; the Revolutionary
Guard
the Guardian Council (Iran), 37

Haghighatjoo, Fatemeh, 136n14
Haghighi, Ashgar, 3
Haj Kazem (Najafi), 56–58
Halqeh-ye Honari, 39
hard-liners, 14, 66, 77, 114–15, 119
Hashemi, Hossein, 130n1
Hatamikia, Ebrahim, 56
heroism, 13, 23, 52, 56, 94, 110. *See also*
masculinity; military (Iran); propa-
ganda; soldiers; veterans
Hezbollah (Lebanon), 6, 34
Hezbollahi, 12–14, 21, 27, 34, 66, 73,
78. *See also* the Basij; clothing; gen-
erations; youth
hijab, 61, 69, 74, 90, 93, 99, 136n14. *See
also* clothing; women
Howzeh Honari (cultural center), 18,
21, 61, 65, 107–8, 130n1
Hussein (Imam), 59, 94, 100
Hussein, Saddam, 4, 29, 89, 95–96

ideologies, 12, 34–35, 38, 40, 47–48, 76
infrastructure, 36, 132n14
insiders, 2, 55, 73, 76–79. *See also
gheyr-e khodi; khodi*; outsiders
Instagram, 45, 82, 105, 110–11
Iran: borders of, 103, 109–11, 133n21;
defense of, 4–5, 98; economy of,
113–14, 116; enemies of, 95, 115;
future of, 3–4, 47–49, 58, 98–99,
117–19, 136n13; identities of, 97,
104, 107; isolation of, 20, 42, 102,
137n20; military of, 105, 116; narratives of, 58, 69; protection of, 4,
6, 100, 104; representations of, 71,
102, 113–14, 136n17
Iranian Hostage Crisis, 6, 137n20
the Iranian Revolution (1979): creation
of, 34, 41, 51, 82; defense of, 5, 7,
13, 23, 33, 48, 56, 72; goals of, x, 11,
36; history of, 6, 28–30, 70, 132n18,
135n7; slogans of, 2, 31; success of,
1, 4, 25, 86. *See also* the Basij; the
Islamic Republic; monarchism; propaganda; protests; regime (Iranian);
the Revolutionary Guard; the Shah;
slogans
Iranian Students' Confederation, 41
Iran International (network), 43
the Iran-Iraq War: beginning of, 6, 22,
31, 47; dangers of, 4, 68, 111; end
of, 28–30, 36–37, 63, 130n1; and
outside influence, 4, 89; stories of,
8, 20–21, 93–94, 118; support for,
ix, 2, 35, 58, 113; symbolism of, 50,
59, 64–65. *See also* the Basij; battlefields; the Revolutionary Guard;
soldiers; veterans; war
Iraq, 29–32, 84, 89–90, 93–94, 109–10,
134n1
Isfahan, Iran, 17
ISIS, 4, 19, 109–11, 116

Islam, 16, 102, 108, 117
the Islamic Republic: defense of, 13,
    43, 93, 102–3, 108; establishment
    of, 4, 6, 11, 28–31, 95; future of, 14,
    98, 119; opposition to, 24, 27, 70,
    84, 86; propaganda of, 72, 90, 116.
    See also the Basij; Iran; the Iranian
    Revolution (1979); propaganda;
    regime (Iranian); regime cultural
    producers; the Revolutionary
    Guard
Islamic Republic of Iran Broadcasting,
    58, 114
Israel, 74, 85–86, 111, 133n21
Istādeh-im tā ākharin Ghatreh-ye Khun,
    106–8

journalism, 4, 20, 43, 57, 67–80, 109

Karaj, Iran, 20, 33
Kayhan (newspaper), 66, 135n2
Kerman, Iran, 24
Kermani, Mehdi, 33–35
Khāb-e Talkh (Amir-Youssefi), 66
Khalkhali, Sadegh, 17
Khamenei, Ali, 37, 39, 84, 115, 133n18,
    135n5
Khatam al-Anbia, 131n14
Khatami, Mohammad, 15, 37, 136n14
khodi, 2, 55, 74, 76–79, 135n7. *See also*
    gheyr-e khodi; insiders; outsiders
Khomeini, Ayatollah, 6; death of, 37,
    133n18; election of, 28, 84; fears of,
    30–31, 132n18; loyalty to, 28–30,
    33, 60; politics of, 34, 36, 38, 42,
    51, 77, 135n5; support for, 14, 23,
    35, 75. *See also* government (Iran);
    Islam; the Islamic Republic
Khorramshahr, Iran, 29–30, 94
Khuzestan, Iran, 29
Kiarostami, Abbas, 54, 66, 137n20

Kulaei, Elahe, 136n14
Kurds, 29, 33–34

languages, 1, 5, 16, 53, 100, 129n1. *See
    also* Persian (language)
Lasswell, Harold, 132n18
Lazarsfeld, Paul, 132n18
London, United Kingdom, 43
Los Angeles, California, 41–44, 104

Majidi, Majid, 137n20
Majles (Iran), 37
Makhmalbaf, Mohsen, 136n9, 137n20
Mannheim, Karl, 35
Manoto (network), 41, 43
marginalization, 12–13, 27, 77, 81–82
Marsie-e Barā-ye Ashegh (Soleimania),
    62–64
martyrdom, 26, 104, 111. *See also*
    propaganda; soldiers; symbolism;
    veterans
Martyrs Foundation, 52–53, 57–58,
    61, 63
Martyrs Museum, 104
masculinity, 98, 139n18
Mashhad, Iran, 115
Masoud, 47
media: censorship of, 5, 23, 43; conflict
    and, x, 10, 114; funding and, 42, 44,
    114, 118; politics and, x, 1, 20, 37,
    86; production of, 1, 41, 97, 110,
    117; strategies of, ix, 10, 22, 75;
    technologies of, 43, 117; Western,
    16, 40, 42–44, 79, 132n18. *See also*
    culture; filmmaking; propaganda;
    regime cultural producers; social
    media
Memories for all Seasons (Karimi), 95,
    138n6
mental illness, 62–64, 83. *See also*
    veterans

Middle East, 6–7, 19, 21–22, 41, 99, 111
military (Iran): culture and, 59, 105;
    politics and, 4, 36–37, 52, 119; and
    training, 9–10, 31–32, 38. *See also*
    the Basij; the Iran-Iraq War; the
    Revolutionary Guard; soldiers
Ministry of Culture and Islamic
    Guidance, 58, 71
Ministry of Intelligence (Iran), 85
Mohammadi, Mostafa, 87, 89
Molāghat Poshteh Divār-hā-ye Ashraf
    (Payeshenas), 138n5
monarchism, 6, 13, 28–30, 43. *See also*
    Shah
Montazeri, Hussein-Ali, 135n5
morality, 37, 101. *See also* hard-liners;
    social life
Mossadegh, Mohammad, 17, 68, 72,
    131n5
mostaz'afin, 29
Mousavi, Mir Hossein, 2–3, 8, 85–86
Mujaheddin-e Khalq organization
    (MEK), 42–44, 75, 83–96, 138n4
music, 37, 44, 63, 76, 96–97, 102–9,
    138n7, ix

Najafi, Masoud, 56
Narrative Foundation, 60
National Company of Construction,
    132n14
National Front, 42
National Iranian Oil Company, 131n5
nationalism, 5–7, 13, 22, 28–30, 33,
    100–106, 117. *See also* propaganda;
    soldiers; veterans
the Netherlands, 44
9 Dey, 115
9/11 (attack), 19
"Nuclear Energy" (Tataloo), 105–6

Obama, Barack, 44
oil, 2, 4, 22, 29, 108, 131n5, 131n14. *See
    also* Abadan, Iran
Open Society, 44
oppression, 9, 31, 59, 100. *See also* mar-
    ginalization; policing; prisoners;
    social life
Organization for Islamic Propagation
    (OIP), 61
outsiders, 2, 16, 54, 66, 73, 76–79,
    135n6. *See also gheyr-e khodi;* insid-
    ers; *khodi;* marginalization

Pahlavi, Mohammad Reza, 6, 132n18
Panahi, Jafar, 66, 74, 137n20
Parastui, Parviz, 56–58
Payeshenas, Morteza, 87, *88,* 89, 91–95,
    99, 138n5
Persian (language), 18, 41, 43–44,
    129n1
Persian Gulf, 104–8, 140n6
policing, 2, 15, 37, 45, 60, 74, 78, 83.
    See also the Basij; censorship; cloth-
    ing; protests; women
politics: conflict and, 16–17, 30–31,
    36, 56, 114, 119; corruption
    and, 2, 64, 95, 116; elections
    and, 38, 107, 115; Islam and, 7,
    33, 110; participation in, 7, 11,
    70, 76, 117; power and, 13, 82,
    111–12; suppression and, 18, 43,
    74; Western influence on, 4, 6,
    14, 28–30, 75, 84, 86, 116, 118.
    See also government (Iran); the
    Green Movement
post-traumatic stress disorder (PTSD),
    62–64. *See also* mental illness;
    veterans
pride, 2, 23, 26, 33–34, 56, 82, 103. *See*

also nationalism; regime (Iranian); symbolism

prisoners, 17, 27, 42, 50, 67, 130n1, 134n1

propaganda: as brainwashing, 89–90; campaigns of, 107–8; dismissal of, 5, 7, 56, 72, 114, 116; distribution of, 117; economics of, 65; effects of, 132n18; production of, 5, 85, 91, 97; and recruitment, 59–60; stories as, 2, 5, 76, 110–11; types of, ix, x, 41, 50–51, 73, 129n4; war and, 34, 52, 64. *See also* media; state television; symbolism

protests: 2009, 2–9, 12–19, 28, 34, 49, 68–69, 74–76, 83, 134n1; 2017, 113–15; 2018, 117. *See also* activism; government (Iran); the Green Movement (2009); the Islamic Republic; Mujaheddin-e Khalq organization (MEK); policing; politics

Qalibaf, Baqer, 103

Quds Special Forces, 109

the Qur'an, 30–31, 40. *See also* faith; Islam

Qur'an Channel, 40, 55

Radio Farda, 41, 43–44

Radio Free Europe, 41

Radio Israel Farsi, 44

Radio Liberty, 41

Rafsanjani, Hashemi, 36

raids, 17, 43. *See also* the Basij; fear; policing

Rajai, Mohammad Ali, 84

RajaNews, 66, 72–73, 135n2

Rajavi, Maryam, 84, 89

Rajavi, Masoud, 84

reformists, 14, 26–27, 38, 77, 99, 112

regime (Iranian): culture and the, 73, 81, 115; definitions of the, 7, 9, 15, 77, 116; opposition to the, 63–64, 72–73, 111, 115, 117; promotion of the, 14, 61, 80, 91, 93, 119; supporters of the, 12–15, 74. *See also* Iran; the Islamic Republic

regime cultural producers, 1, 7–9, 14–26, 47, 55, 60, 66, 72–82, 91–96, 102–9, 117–18. *See also* the Basij; filmmaking; propaganda; state television

regime media producers, x, 7, 20–25, 41–45, 64, 102–6, 110, 114–19. *See also* the Basij; filmmaking; propaganda; state television

Revāyat-e Fath (Avini), 59

Revāyat-e Fath Center, 21, 26

revolutionaries, 6, 26, 30, 60, 75, 82, 135n6

the Revolutionary Guard: as career, 1, 23–24, 33, 38, 45; challenges of, 14, 30–33, 36–37; creation of, 29, 36, 47; generations of the, 2–3; influence of, ix, x, 2, 21, 37, 40, 112, 114; leaders of the, 5, 10; members of, 13, 19, 27; as protector, 61, 101–2, 106–7, 109; representations of, 7, 16, 20, 34, 110; wealth of, 46, 131n14. *See also* the Basij; the Iran-Iraq War; military (Iran); protests; soldiers; veterans; war

Rouhani, Hassan, 113–15

rowshanfekrs, 79, 136n17, 137n17

Rule of Jurisprudence (Khomeini), 133n18

Saadatabad Psychiatric Wellness Center, 62
"Sacred Defense" films, 87
Sacred Defense Garden and Museum, 102–4
Sadr Psychiatric Hospital, 62
Salesman (Farhadi), 137n20
Sarhangi, Morteza, 4
satellite television, 21, 43–45, 69, 79–80, 104–5, 114–16. *See also* journalism; media; state television
Saudi Arabia, 85–86, 102, 111, 117
sāzmān-e tablighāt-e islāmi, 61
scholarship, 7, 16, 20. *See also* ethnography; fieldwork (ethnographic)
A Separation (Farhadi), 137n20
the Shah: ousting of, 2, 6, 28–31, 42, 68, 75, 84, 133n18; rule of, 17, 78, 102, 131n5
Shāhnāmeh (Ferdowsi), 101, 108
Shariatmadari, Hossein, 135n2
Shefah, Mohammad Reza, 107
Shiraz, Iran, 110
Shirazi, Alireza, 5
slogans, 2, 30–31, 115–16. *See also* the Green Movement (2009); the Iranian Revolution (1979); protests
smartphones, 42, 72, 97, 117. *See also* social media
Sobhani, Mohammad Hussein, 93
social life: factions of, 2, 35; policing of, 11, 15, 37, 48–49, 117; and privacy, 83, 138n1; values of, 12, 25, 37–38, 135n3. *See also* clothing; families; protests
social media, 44–45, 97, 105, 107–11, 113–15
soft war, 39, 44, 79, 133n21. *See also* culture; media; United States; war

soldiers: heroism of, 108, 111; recruitment of, 34, 46, 59, 64; as volunteers, 9–10, 23, 29, 31–33, 56, 59. *See also* the Basij; battlefields; Iraq; military (Iran); propaganda; the Revolutionary Guard; state television; United States; veterans; war
Soleimani, 110
Soleimani, Qassim, 109–12
Soleimania, Ahmad, 62–64
spirituality, 28, 59. *See also* faith; Islam; the Qur'an
state television: boredom with, 94, 101; censorship by, 53–54, 63–64, 93; films of, 5, 22, 28, 39–40, 53, 130n3, 138n8; stories of, 73, 94, 113. *See also* filmmaking; the Islamic Republic; media; propaganda
storytelling: censorship of, 25, 51–53, 56; film as, 87–88; ongoing, 18, 73, 116–17; as propaganda, 1–5, 11, 19, 93, 116; traditions of, 63, 95, 97, 100–101, 103. *See also* families; film festivals; filmmaking; heroism; media; symbolism; veterans
students: and the Basij, 39–42, 67, 70, 75; politics of, 6, 9–12, 20–24, 84, 92–94, 110–11; relationships between, 81, 103, 138n23. *See also* "Art Circle" (university organization); the Basij; clothing; universities
Stuxnet Cyberattacks, 85–86
the Supreme Leader: politics of, 2, 27, 36, 39, 44, 114, 116; support of, 61, 107, 135n2. *See also* Islam; the Islamic Republic
Sureh magazine, 130n1
Sureh Publishing House, 65, 76, 108

Sureh-ye Mehr, 21

symbolism, 51–56, 102, 104–6, 108.
    See also Iran; media; propaganda;
    regime (Iranian); regime cultural
    producers; regime media produc-
    ers; storytelling; veterans; war

Syria, 3–4, 31, 83, 85–86, 109–10

Tasnim, 66

Tasnim News Agency, 135n2

Tataloo, Amir, 105–6

Tehran, Iran: art in, 1, 20–21, 49, 61,
    84, 87, 96, 102–3; conditions of, 6,
    18, 26, 65, 71; immigration to, 9,
    24–25

Telegram, 44, 105, 110–11

terrorism, 19–20, 84. *See also*
    Mujaheddin-e Khalq organization
    (MEK); 9/11 (attack)

Toronto, Canada, 43

travel, 18, 46, 51, 57, 79, 91, 97, 117–18,
    137n17. *See also* Europe; youth

Trump, Donald, 44

Tudeh Party, 42

Turkey, 43

unemployment, 29, 113. *See also* eco-
    nomics; Iran; politics

*An Unfinished Film for My Daughter
    Somayeh* (Payeshenas), 87–95, 88,
    138n5

United Arab Emirates (UAE), 43

United States: and foreign policy, 6–7,
    14, 19, 28–30, 102, 131n5; and
    influence, 6, 19, 39; and the MEK,
    84–86; military of, 90, 107–9, 111,
    133n21, 140n6

universities, 10, 19, 21, 39, 81, 136n17.
    See also "Art Circle" (university

organization); the Basij; students;
    specific universities

University of Tehran, 34, 110–11

Velayat-e Faqih (Khomeini), 73, 133n18

veterans: care for, 23, 57–58, 62–64,
    83, 113; lives of, x, 8, 16, 24,
    51–54, 56, 121. *See also* the Basij;
    heroism; the Iran-Iraq War; mar-
    ginalization; martyrdom; Martyrs
    Foundation; mental illness;
    military (Iran); the Revolutionary
    Guard; soldiers

*Visitation behind the Walls of Camp
    Ashraf* (Payeshenas), 138n5

Voice of America (VOA), 41, 44

volunteerism, 9, 23, 29–32, 56, 59–60.
    See also the Basij; families; the Iran-
    Iraq War; Martyrs Foundation;
    military (Iran); propaganda; the
    Revolutionary Guard; soldiers; vet-
    erans; youth

war: culture of, 4, 35, 44, 55; dangers of,
    4, 42, 52, 121; depictions of, 50–51,
    53–54, 59–60, 103–4; and heroism,
    23, 93–94; narratives of, 22, 28–30,
    33, 56, 94, 118, 130n1; symbol-
    ism of, 31, 59–60; and Western
    influence, 7, 30, 95, 102–3. *See
    also* the Basij; the Iran-Iraq War;
    military (Iran); propaganda; the
    Revolutionary Guard; soldiers; state
    television; veterans

War Films Bureau, 58

War Group Team, 58

"We Are Standing until the Last Drop
    of Blood," 106–8

Williams, Raymond, 98

The Wolves, 95
women: clothing and, 8, 10–11, 18, 24,
    61, 90, 108, 136n13, 138n3; expec-
    tations of, 67, 72, 77–78; fears of,
    37, 90, 121, 135n3; limitations of,
    19, 48, 98–99, 118, 136n14; piety of,
    16, 18. *See also* censorship; families;
    policing; politics
World War I, 132n18

youth: alienation of, 3, 45; appeals to,
    11, 25, 100–101, 116; corruption
    of, 39, 94, 133n18; as hezbol-
    lahi, 12–13, 103, 117; media and,
    47, 104, 117. *See also* the Basij;
    families; generations; protests;
    social media; soldiers; universities;
    volunteerism
YouTube, 110. *See also* social media

Hicham Safieddine, *Banking on the State: The Financial Foundations of Lebanon*
2019

Chiara De Cesari, *Heritage and the Cultural Struggle for Palestine*
2019

Sara Pursley, *Familiar Futures: Time, Selfhood, and Sovereignty in Iraq*
2019

Tareq Baconi, *Hamas Contained: The Rise and Pacification of Palestinian Resistance*
2018

Begüm Adalet, *Hotels and Highways: The Construction of Modernization Theory in Cold War Turkey*
2018

Elif M. Babül, *Bureaucratic Intimacies: Translating Human Rights in Turkey*
2017

Orit Bashkin, *Impossible Exodus: Iraqi Jews in Israel*
2017

Maha Nassar, *Brothers Apart: Palestinian Citizens of Israel and the Arab World*
2017

Asef Bayat, *Revolution without Revolutionaries: Making Sense of the Arab Spring*
2017

Nahid Siamdoust, *Soundtrack of the Revolution: The Politics of Music in Iran*
2017

Laure Guirguis, *Copts and the Security State: Violence, Coercion, and Sectarianism in Contemporary Egypt*
2016

Michael Farquhar, *Circuits of Faith: Migration, Education, and the Wahhabi Mission*
2016

Gilbert Achcar, *Morbid Symptoms: Relapse in the Arab Uprising*
2016

Jacob Mundy, *Imaginative Geographies of Algerian Violence: Conflict Science, Conflict Management, Antipolitics*
2015

Ilana Feldman, *Police Encounters: Security and Surveillance in Gaza under Egyptian Rule*
2015

Tamir Sorek, *Palestinian Commemoration in Israel: Calendars, Monuments, and Martyrs*
2015

Adi Kuntsman and Rebecca L. Stein, *Digital Militarism: Israel's Occupation in the Social Media Age*
2015

Laurie A. Brand, *Official Stories: Politics and National Narratives in Egypt and Algeria*
2014

Kabir Tambar, *The Reckonings of Pluralism: Citizenship and the Demands of History in Turkey*
2014

Diana Allan, *Refugees of the Revolution: Experiences of Palestinian Exile*
2013

Shira Robinson, *Citizen Strangers: Palestinians and the Birth of Israel's Liberal Settler State*
2013